The Long Road of War

The Long Road of War

A Marine's Story of Pacific Combat

James W. Johnston

University of Nebraska Press
Lincoln and London

© 1998 by the University
of Nebraska Press
All rights reserved
Manufactured in the United
States of America
⊗ The paper in this book
meets the minimum
requirements of
American National Standard
for Information Sciences —
Permanence of Paper for
Printed Library Materials,
ANSI Z39.48-1984.
Library of Congress
Cataloging-in-Publication Data
Johnston, James W., 1922–
The long road of war :
a marine's story of Pacific
combat / James W. Johnston.
    p.   cm.
Includes bibliographical references.
ISBN 0-8032-2585-7 (cl : alk. paper)
    1. Johnston, James W., 1922–   .
    2. World War, 1939–1945—
    Campaigns—Pacific Area.
3. World War, 1939–1945—Personal
    narratives, American.
4. United States.   Marine Corps—Biography.
    5. Soldiers—United States—Biography.
        I. Title.
        D767.9.J65   1998
940.54′26—dc21   97–23894
        CIP

To my family, and to the brave men I knew

Contents

Illustrations

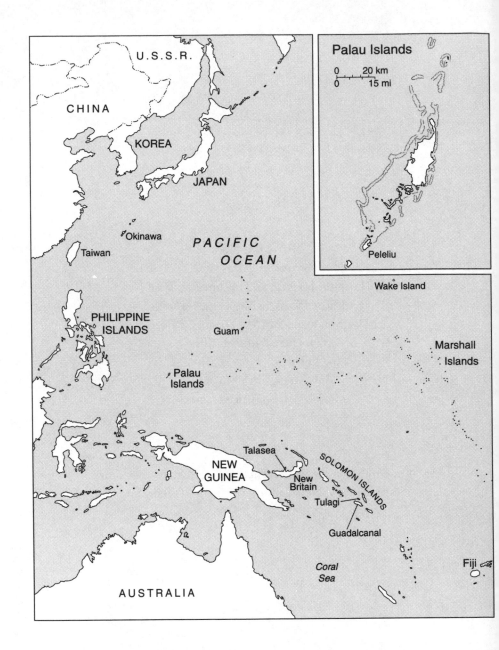

Areas of combat in the Pacific Theater discussed by the author:
New Guinea, New Britain, Peleliu, and Okinawa

Foreword

IN HIS MEMORABLE self-description, Jim Johnston was a "flat-trajectory" marine. That is, as a machine gunner in the Fifth Marine Regiment of the First Marine Division, he was directly on the front lines, fully exposed to the enemy's flat-trajectory small arms fire, with no buffer between him and the Japanese troops trying to kill him — and whom he, in turn, wanted to kill.

In World War II (as in subsequent wars), flat-trajectory soldiers were a doubly endangered subset of the human species, first because of their small numbers and second because of their precarious, exposed position. Only a comparative handful of soldiers ever experienced the enemy's flat-trajectory gunfire. Most military personnel were in rear areas or in combat support units, and by Jim's reckoning these folks had it relatively easy. Even marine mortarmen only a few hundred yards behind the front were usually beyond the enemy's rifle range and thus, as Jim asserts, they avoided "the constant exposure to flat-trajectory fire that was the daily and nightly fare of our riflemen and machine gunners." Few in numbers to begin with, front-line soldiers faced extinction once the fighting began. During the horrific Pacific island campaigns on New Britain, Peleliu, and Okinawa, Jim's squad had 300 percent casualties and a mortality rate of more than 83 percent.

With personal survival constantly at stake, a combat soldier perceives the world differently than ordinary people. The well-ordered chronology and concise measurements of time and distance that so clearly dominate the lives of civilians and the uniformed personnel at the rear are meaningless to those on the front lines, where all is jumble and chaos. As the reader will discover, the "facts" in a true war story are uncommonly ambiguous and opaque, often remembered in isolated fragments jerked out of their context by the vagaries of memory, a memory that has endured unendurable stress.

In combat, Jim almost never knew exactly *where* he was, or precisely *when* he was wherever he was. Nor did the high command ever bother explaining to him how his unit's activities fit into the larger tactical situation. And since somebody was trying to kill him every day, day in and day out, he did not care whether he had been wounded on a Tuesday or a Saturday — only whether he would live. As for distance, whether he had to move a few meters or a few miles was unimportant. What mattered was whether he could traverse the distance, however far it might be, and still be alive when he reached his destination, wherever it was. How long did it take to get there? A few minutes? A couple of hours? Days? Jim did not really care; however long it took, he just wanted to see at least one more sunrise, and then another, and still another.

During his travails Jim made several disconcerting discoveries, which every combat soldier learns. First, despite the alleged sanctity of the individual in American society, the military high command considered Jim akin to a gallon of gasoline: just another expendable commodity to be consumed in pursuit of a larger goal. Second, killing all too often brought not remorse but a satisfying exhilaration, and the greater the slaughter, the greater the satisfaction. Most profoundly, in combat Jim was fighting *not* for the United States of America or democracy or the Four Freedoms, not even for Mom, apple pie, or the girl down the street. Foxhole concerns were more intensely immediate: he fought "for the guys sitting in the hole with [him]. You do things you didn't believe you could make yourself do because you don't want to let them down." Since those fellow foxhole wallowers felt the same way, they were all fighting for their mutual personal survival. Everything else, well, screw it.

Survivors among flat-trajectory soldiers, like Jim Johnston, are first of all a very small blood fraternity — a rare breed, like whooping cranes and giant pandas. They are also fundamentally different from all other Homo sapiens, those billions who have never been part of the grisly human-meat-grinder that history innocuously labels "a battle," where the trappings of civilization and the luxuries of morality and ideology count for exactly zero. Jim acknowledges that he may now look like an ordinary man walking down the sidewalk, but he knows that deep inside he is not. Despite his seemingly normal exterior and the passage of more than fifty years, he remains "much closer to the jungle than to the city street," afflicted with hellish recurring nightmares, and bitterly angry about "the criminal sickness that is war, and the terrible, unimaginable human behavior that is found there."

He has, Jim writes, told "the unadorned and unaltered truth." He might have added the word "unpleasant," because his honest, unfiltered unpleasantness makes *The Long Road of War* enthralling reading for those who want to understand combat and what it does to flat-trajectory troops, at the time of battle and thereafter.

Peter Maslowski

Preface

I HAVE MIXED EMOTIONS about setting to paper the memories of my time in the United States Marine Corps, just as I have mixed emotions about the corps itself. I refer to them as memories, rather than memoirs, since the latter term seems a bit high-flown, something better left to politicians or generals.

Three considerations led me, at last, to take pen in hand and write. First is the undoubtedly futile hope that by showing these memories the light of day I might somehow mitigate the sights and sounds of a war fought fifty years ago — sights and sounds that are with me yet and that will accompany me to the grave.

Second is the fact that I have read some accounts of campaigns in which I took part, written by various authors with varying credentials, that I believe are not entirely correct. As a consequence, I feel compelled to recount those events I witnessed with my own eyes.

Third is the urgings of friends and family, without whose aid and encouragement I'm sure this project could not have been completed.

I have not written a historical narrative. There are already a number of books concerning the Pacific Theater of the World War II, and each can serve to illuminate the reader regarding overall strategies, troop movements, and the like. Rather, I have written to recount a human experience, the experience of a combat veteran who was on the ground in the midst of the conflict, one who was not privy to much of the grand scheme of the enterprise and whose duty dictated an urgent preoccupation with the waging of war on more personal terms.

I joined the Marine Corps a few days after my twentieth birthday. Through the days and months and years I served with the marines, I wrote frequent letters home to my folks. As chance would have it, my mother saved those letters. They are almost a story in themselves, in spite of the government's censorship of the letters and in spite of my own attempts to protect my mother in her helpless position by hiding or soft-pedaling many things. I quote the letters here both for what they contain and as a guide to help me remember all the things they couldn't say. I will fill in what was implied between the lines and what was lived between the letters to convey the story of my outfit in World War II.

I have, from time to time throughout my life, heard veterans of some wars speak disparagingly about veterans of others. Men of war (be it Vietnam, Korea, World War II, World War I, or any other damn war) who look with disdain upon other men of war for some imagined differences between them reflect either their own lack of intelligence or their own lack of honesty. By their prejudice they shine light on their own shortcomings.

If war is seen in the form of a fraction, the numerator in the fraction is different from war to war, outfit to outfit, day to day, hill to hill, but there is a common denominator. That denominator is the human experience of physical exhaustion and pain, deprivation, and the mental anguish of confusion, sadness, and dread.

In the midst of battle, what the world may think of you is generally the farthest thing from your mind. I have had many good laughs over a story that a dear friend of mine, a World War I veteran, told me about a comrade of his. They were in France under a prolonged enemy artillery barrage. During a brief pause in the barrage, my friend's buddy turned to him and said, "If I live through this, I'll never love another damn country."

What happens to each individual soldier that is personally critical to him is much the same in one war as it is in every other. The true warrior, in experience, finds that the Halls of Glory are really the Horrors of War, and he feels, deprived of the benefits of civilized society and in mortal danger, that he is not in the same game with the rest of his countrymen. Whether you call him a dummy or a hero when he gets home doesn't make one cubit of difference in his stature. Neither does it wipe out the nightmares nor bring back dead friends.

I was in E Company, Second Battalion, Fifth Marines. This is the Marine Corps designation for one of the rifle companies in the Fifth Regiment. The Fifth is one of the infantry regiments of the First Marine Division (the first one, incidentally, despite the inconsistency of numbering). Though I always think of it as the best outfit ever assembled, in my heart I realize that I am biased. Most rifle company personnel I knew thought of their unit as the best. Officer and NCO cadres were all-important and in the corps they were generally very competent. The counterfeits seldom lasted long. Rifle companies (we usually called them line companies) all had much in common. If you didn't have a lot of spirit, self-confidence, and pride, a line company in the marines was the wrong place for you.

A rifle company, any rifle company, is humanity's last ditch. Everyone who is familiar with the role of infantry in war knows that what I say is true: A rifle company is humanity's last ditch. The line companies are almost always subjected to the most prolonged and costly combat, and the nature of their lousy job is unremitting physical and mental abuse. The great masses of those companies are men who are for all practical purposes the same, and they experience an almost complete loss of individuality. As a matter of fact, most outfits (the Marine Corps among them) cultivate the destruction of individuality.

My entire association with the Marine Corps is one of ambivalence. I have profound and abiding admiration for, and appreciation of, the men with whom I served. I also have a complete lack of regard for, or even tolerance of, the capricious abuse of both privilege and authority that is so prevalent in the Marine Corps organization. That abuse of power was well recognized by the enlisted men of the corps, and they referred to it by a typically earthy term — chickenshit. It is born of the frailty of a premise in which some human beings (who are subject, like us all, to human jealousy and human ignorance) are given, by rank, almost unrestrained authority over others. Anyone who is given the omnipotence that rank has over subordinates should also have the omniscient qualities required to administer that power properly.

I realize that it's a Catch-22 situation. Without powerful authority over them, some men will abuse the lack of control. Conversely, with limitless authority over others, some men will abuse the use of control. However, as it operates in wartime, the military caste system is the maker of many a sad iniquity.

It was my good fortune to serve with many a truly sterling officer — some commissioned and some noncommissioned. It was also my sad misfortune to be associated with some who, by any standard of fitness, should long before have been mustered out of the corps.

In the years since the war I have read all I can that has been written by authors who were in frontline battle; pitched battle; close, mortal encounters.

Some of the authors write of blackout times, times when they must have walked past their dead or wounded buddies, but they can't remember seeing what was in front of them. Perhaps some physiological or psychological phenomenon of nature is protecting them.

My experience was almost the exact opposite. I remember, as if it were etched into my brain, the blue and yellow distension of Lamm's thigh, torn apart inside when the bullet went in through his knee and came out his back. I see, almost as if I were still holding him, the exposed part of Lacaria's backbone where the shrapnel had gouged a strip across his back.

If I close my eyes and think the name Brown, I can see the burst intestine hanging out the hole where his leg had been blown off, almost as if it had been pulled out by the roots.

There are some people named Carman who live near my present home. When I hear the name in the course of everyday conversation, I often think of the body of the boy who lay beside me, his face looking up at the sky from between his feet, his back broken and his body arched completely over, backward.

Probably the one I see plainest, the most indelible one, is Himmelsbach, my close friend, when I held his head with my hand and watched the blood ooze out the holes in his abdomen, and felt the surge of his gasps, and life leave his body.

I still see the stub of one guy's leg; the stub of another guy's arm; the dull, blind eyes of another.

I have five dreams that recur through the years. They run and rerun like the reels of a movie. In the first dream the mortars are landing in the high grass on the gentle slopes on New Britain, and the smoke is oozing from the cracks in Mother Earth's surface where the big shells have landed.

The second dream is of the screaming of the bombs as they fall toward us from the Mitsubishi bombers. I awaken just before the bombs land and blow us all to hell. I see ads on American TV saying "Mitsubishi," a word that is becoming more familiar in our society. They are trying to build confidence in their product among the new American acquaintances who are ignorant or indifferent. To me they do not have to familiarize their name. I still wake up in the middle of the night with my mind silently screaming, "Mitsubishis, Mitsubishis, Mitsubishis."

The third dream is of the silhouette of the first Jap I shot with my pistol. In reality he went down immediately. In my dreams, however, I keep shooting him but he won't die — he just keeps coming.

Dream four is the Japs charging at us on Peleliu, screaming "BANZAI!" as they came. They had bayonets fixed on the end of long poles. Somehow, in reality, we got them stopped, killing them all before they reached us. In my dreams we can't stop them and I awaken just as the bayonet starts into my belly.

The fifth and final dream is about the causeway on Peleliu where I keep trying to move forward but the Jap machine guns and snipers kill the marines around me too fast for us to advance. Each time I see the little geysers of water and puffs of dust where the bullets from the automatic weapons hit all around me.

RESIDUAL

You little yellow men I see your faces
Now and then throughout the passing years,
Long since your friends have settled in their places
And loved ones shed the last of all their tears.

Long since the death of love's last smoldering ember,
After those you knew have ceased to weep,
I from this far land must still remember —
I see your faces here before me sleep.

And so I shall tell you my story. The story of the war and the men and the Marine Corps that I knew. What I will tell you, as I know and believe it, is the unadorned and unaltered truth.

James W. Johnston

The Long Road of War

1. My Introduction to the Corps

SINCE I CAN REMEMBER, most everyone has called me Jim. Sometimes Jimmie, and once in a while Jim Bill, but never James. I was born on December 13, 1922, in a house built mostly of logs. I was brought into this world by a dear man named Dr. Atkinson, who attended my mother at the old family farmhouse in the Cumberland Mountains (perhaps more accurately described as the Cumberland Plateau of the Appalachian Mountains) in Adair County, southern Kentucky.

I was christened James for my paternal great-grandfather Johnston; William for my maternal great-grandfather William Penn Ferguson. I remember hearing Civil War stories in my earliest recollections, for my father and his family (native Kentuckians) sympathized with the South, and my mother (whose grandfather lost the use of an arm to a Confederate rifle ball while serving with the Fourth Pennsylvania Volunteer Cavalry) had her own respects. She often sang to me, when only she and I were present:

> Sherman's dashing Yankee boys will never reach the coast,
> So the saucy rebels said and 'twas a haughty boast,
> Had they not forgot, alas, to reckon with the host,
> While we were marching through Georgia.

Dear reader, I can almost hear you say, "And so, Jim Johnston, where did *your* sympathies lie?" To which I could only reply:

> Under the sod and the dew,
> Waiting the judgement day; —

Love and tears, for the Blue;
Tears and love, for the Gray.
(from *The Blue and The Gray* by F. M. Finch)

My family moved to Wauneta, a small town in southwest Nebraska, when I was very young. (My mother's family had homesteaded in that area shortly after the turn of the century.) That is where I grew up. The folks moved back to Kentucky during the war but returned to Nebraska just before the war was over.

Wauneta is located in the beautiful little Frenchman Creek valley. The town had its beginning near a set of falls in the river that was used later to power a mill and, still later, turbines to supply electricity. On the tablelands on both sides of the valley are large, fertile areas of farmland. Through the dust bowl days the lack of rain and depressed crop prices caused serious hardships for the farmers and for the little town that was dependent on them for its very existence. Many farmers lost their land because they couldn't pay the property taxes. The hardiest survived, however, and the town grew to several hundred people.

When I was still in grade school, my beloved older brother, Joshua, was killed in a hunting accident. He was five years my senior and from my earliest recollections had sought to be a buffer between me and the world's harsher aspects.

He was very intelligent and also very adept at making things with his hands. He was at the head of his class and he built intricate things of wood. (I still treasure a checkerboard he made in manual training at school.)

He was especially kind to and considerate of me. He helped me with my schooling and would always take the time to help me in any other way that he could. He was so much more talented than I in most every way that in jealous anger I would sometimes assail him, but he never reacted meanly. It would have been easy for him to manhandle me, but he never did. He would just hold me at arm's length until I cooled off. One time, in one of my misguided fits of anger, I threw a piece of steel at him. It hit him in the head and hurt him rather badly. I have never gotten over my shame for doing so.

He was my only sibling and was so much a part of my life that when he was killed I felt as though the world had ended. It was many months after his death before I began to be reconciled that life must go on. Through the years, and still, Josh was and is often in my thoughts.

I was, for the most part, a typical smalltown boy, I guess. My generation came up through the Depression, and though there was never a lot of money around, we pretty much had the run of the place. I liked cars and motorcycles, pool halls and ball games. The soda fountain was a popular hangout, and when we could scrape together the ten-cent admission, there was a movie theater in town. After I got older, like most young guys, I had a decided inclination toward young girls and I enjoyed the Saturday night dances.

I first went to school in an old wooden building that accommodated both grade school and high school. When I was in the fourth or fifth grade the schoolhouse burned down. We held class in the basement of the Methodist church while the town built a new brick schoolhouse. It was a great asset for those times but pretty modest by today's standards. The gymnasium where I learned to play basketball was about one-fourth regulation size, and the out-of-bounds lines were just a foot from the concrete walls of the gym.

I liked school and was a pretty good student. For what it's worth, I was valedictorian of my high school class and had academic scholarships to several colleges. I didn't have a passion for any particular academic pursuit, and I hadn't set any specific career goals, but I was interested in engineering and geology. (One of my scholarship offers was to the Colorado School of Mines.)

I was of medium height with a slim build, not much like the specimens you see on recruiting posters, but I had pretty good physical skills. I had reasonably good foot speed and strength (for my size), and my reflexes and eyes were a little above average, I think. I had earned nineteen varsity letters in academics and a variety of sports in four years of high school, and I was later offered a basketball scholarship to a small junior college in Nebraska.

I had enrolled at the University of Nebraska–Lincoln but I didn't want to stay in ROTC or the reserves with a war going on, so I quit school. When I joined the marines I requested duty with the Fleet Marine Force, which is basically the infantry divisions of the corps, because I thought it was the honorable thing to do. After a few weeks in the States I was sent overseas, and I stayed there until the last blitz of the war was over. During that time, after having been given the responsibility of a small command, I never sent a man anywhere in combat that I didn't go with him. In the event I sent two or more men in different directions, I went with the one I thought would need me most. Those words can be quickly and easily written now, but to be able to state them honestly I lived many months of loneliness, fear, despondency, and a certain amount of bloody pain. I am thankful that I was able to hang together through those days. In many ways I am not sorry for the time I spent there, and in many ways I am.

Hemingway wrote, "There is no hunting like the hunting of man, and those who have hunted armed men long enough and like it, never care for anything else thereafter." I don't know if I completely agree with him, but I do know this: Though I didn't realize it at the time, when I had finished signing all those enlistment papers that day in Denver, Colorado, *I had committed the rest of my life*, whether or not I lived through the war. After you have once been in the corps through the guts of a war — if you spent enough months or years there to get used to it — you should never get out, for you are never again as you were before. Nor are you ever again the same as the rest of the people in civilized society. You walk down the street looking much the same as other people walking down the street, but you do not feel or think the same. Most of the traditional social, moral, and economic conventions are ludicrous to you. You pray that you will be able to maintain a behavior that will keep you out of trouble in a normal, peaceful society without compromising too much of what you believe. You are, inside, much closer to the jungle than to the city street.

Through the years I have learned to say a few prayers that have been satisfying in battle and out. Mostly I say the Lord's Prayer and I believe that would suffice on about any occasion. I say a few others, too, because I can't help it.

One prayer is of gratitude for my life and the chance to do with it what I will. Another is of hope that I may die like a man and not leave too much of a mess for having been here. And I pray a prayer for which many sanctimonious (perhaps righteous) people would probably condemn me: "Father, I thank thee for good whiskey and pretty girls, for beautiful music, good food, and plenty of precious water. I pray it's OK for me to enjoy them, for I came too close to missing them all to pass them by now."

I have read some of the works of Siegfried Sassoon and James Jones, and I have often thought how much I would love to talk to them. Unfortunately, I cannot, for they are gone. Though I do not consider myself an author of their ability, I am sure there will be *some* people who will want to talk to me, out of love, or hate, or curiosity. If only I can get this finished in time for them to read before I am gone.

The first card I wrote home is postmarked January 6, 1943.

> Dearest Mom and Dad,
>
> It is 2:30 Wednesday. We are on the train almost to Albuquerque, New Mexico. We won't stop long (15 min.) so will have to hurry. Everything is swell. Nice weather. The watch runs fine now, Dad. Will be in San Diego tomorrow. I'll write the next stop. This is the first one of more than 10 minutes.
>
> Jim

I had told them goodbye the night before at the railroad station in Denver. In the afternoon I had signed my name to all the papers required for enlistment and, with four other men, had been sworn into the United States Marine Corps.

A strange aura had pervaded the evening. I had made up my mind and fulfilled the decision. Now there was no turning back. Whatever else, the die was cast. Mother, Dad, and I had eaten a supper prompted solely by habit and punctuated by the short bits of completely inconsequential conversation in which we endeavored to ease the intense sorrow of parting. Thereafter, we had a long, excruciating wait at the station for departure time. We had patted one another on the shoulder and tried to say consoling things. During those few moments, which like the previous days and years had both dragged and flown by, we had watched the others around us in the station. Other people had been preparing, as ineptly as we, to part. The bright lights and the crowds of the city are always in a manner depressing and foreign to a boy from the country. I had been preparing to leave my parents for the first time and quite conceivably for the last time. The idea of the unknown in the new life awaiting me had lent its mystification. I had felt the human family's natural aversion to change — a feeling that is close kin to the fear of death. I had been loosed from my moorings to swirl like a leaf in the wind. Many other circumstances had complemented the unearthly atmosphere, but throughout the day, diminishing all other circumstances to the subconscious background, had loomed the imminent, thick, black ugliness of goodbye. Few things in this world approach the poignant drama of railway stations during wartime. Far into his life the serviceman remembers the pew-like seats, the faces of the huge clocks, the droning voice of the loudspeaker, the timetables, and, above all, the last longing look out the coach window at the helpless, kind, and loving faces that he leaves behind. How many final adieus were thus said? How many life stories were to read, "The association of his life and mine ended in a farewell at the railway station in Denver. Before we could meet again, one of us would be no more"?

When the train cleared the station it ran slowly through the switchyards. Up the banks that rose on both sides of the yards stood the little, dingy smoke-colored shacks that were the homes of people whom society relegates to such places. As we passed through the area I saw a large cleared area where some enterprising operator had bought a bunch of lots and had torn down the shacks on them in order to build a nightclub. The neon lights that ran all the way around the club shone on the tops of the cars that packed the parking area. Inside, people would be toasting the town, dancing, living it up. For a moment I felt the call of adventure. Then the train started to pick up speed, and the lights along the track started to thin out. In a little while, we went through Englewood and I looked back at the twinkling lights of Denver. I was on my way down a long road.

It was then that I began to take notice of the individuality of my companions. The five of us who were sworn in that afternoon had been joined by a pair that had been sworn in previously, making seven in all. We introduced ourselves to one another and started to exchange short personal histories in a hurried-up way of making acquaintance. One of the seven (who was, in fact, reenlisting, having served earlier) was wearing a Marine Corps uniform. On his left sleeve were what I later learned to call "one up and one down." On the lower part of his sleeve was one diagonal stripe, a so-called hash mark, signifying that he had served a hitch (four years) in the corps. On his upper sleeve was one chevron, signifying a private first class. He was a sharp guy, though he had attained no higher rank in four years. My education about Marine Corps rating had begun. I soon picked my bunk mate from the bunch, and as I seemed acceptable to him we began a comradeship, a friendship, that grew stronger during the brief time we knew each other. He was one of the other four sworn in that afternoon, and following our basic training we two would be assigned to different units. His name was Robert Stamm, and his young life would end in the Marianas on the island of Saipan.

I will not reproduce in entirety all the letters I wrote home. It is almost unbelievable, and embarrassing to me now, that I could ever have been as naive as the letters reveal me to be. I will, however, try to include parts of enough letters to establish some semblance of chronology and to impart some experiences that may be significant or interesting.

The next letter is postmarked San Bernadino, California, 9:00 P.M., January 7, 1943.

En route to S.D.

Dearest Mom and Dad

Well we're in California now. If we stop in L.A. I will mail this there.

We are in cactus country. The cacti are as big as fairly good-sized trees. The army mechanized units are in maneuvers around here. There are a lot of tank tracks and tin cans around.

These guys are really swell boys. We have bull sessions about every night. One of them plays a mouth harp, and he's pretty good, too.

I just found the letter you wrote, Mom. It kinda surprised me (happily).[1]

I'll write again. There is lots to write about.

Jim

It was obvious that all the guys were apprehensive. We had heard all about what marine boot camp[2] was in those days, and we wondered if we would be able to stand the gaff and produce as was expected and required of us.

I tried with a humble bravado to write trivia and cover my doubts from the folks, unsuccessfully, I am sure. I know they felt my uneasiness. Today, as I read that last letter I wrote on the train going to San Diego, I thought of the many times I awoke in the night as we traveled through the desert Southwest and stared out the train window at the desolation of the darkness. I already felt a million miles away from home, yet my journey had barely begun.

When we got to Dago we disembarked from the train. We were loaded onto buses and hauled to the RDMCB — the recruit depot Marine Corps base. It was located in urban San Diego, but I was never oriented well enough to know what part of the city. There were some permanent, masonry-type buildings with paved streets to accommodate the base personnel. There were also row after row of little rectangular composition-board shacks to house the recruits. (The compo-board, as it was often called, was a cheap sheeting material.) In that area, the paths were deep, loose sand. It was the bleak place that has been so well documented in many books and movies, and it would be our home for the next seven weeks. There we began the equally well-documented rigmarole of marine boot camp.

It seemed as though I had barely laid down late the first night in Dago when I was awakened by a corporal shouting, "OK, you shitheads, hit the deck.[3] Rise and shine."

I opened my eyes. The glare of the bright lights across the underside of the open rafters on the little compo-board hut hit me like stage lights.

The corporal continued his grating, nearly monotonic instructions.

"Make up your sacks. Roll the mattresses against the bulkheads like you found them," and so on. "Be ready to fall out in the company street in five minutes."

I looked at the little silver Gruen wristwatch the folks had given me in Denver. It was 2:15 A.M. The hectic routine that would fill our time for the next few weeks had begun.

By design, the DIS (drill instructors) were insulting and overbearing, but if you acted on the outside like they scared the hell out of you, yet inwardly didn't pay any attention to their harassment, it wasn't bad. Most of it was rather fun. We had one DI who was first-class. He was very efficient and surprisingly kind. When he had charge of the platoon, it was especially fun.

The most difficult and unpleasant part of boot camp was the lack of sufficient time or space to complete some of the duties that were assigned.

We had to wash our clothes with a scrub brush in an area with wooden racks on which to scrub. There were about one-fourth the number of racks necessary for everyone to complete their scrubbing in the time allotted. Because I couldn't figure out any other way to get it done, I would get up in the middle of the night and go use one of the lavatories in the head (latrine) to wash what I couldn't get done during the day. Since I could not put things out to dry before a designated time, I'd wring the clothes out as dry as I could and leave them rolled up in my bucket under my sack. (The bucket, incidentally, was an integral part of boot camp life. It was issued to us when we arrived and had a variety of uses throughout basic training. We were often told to "bring your bucket" or "leave your bucket.") When it came time to wash, I would get the wet clothes out of the bucket and hang them out to dry. It would short me a little on sleep but otherwise it worked great, for a while.

One day a lieutenant inspecting our area saw some socks I'd washed and left in the bucket. He decided that that was out of line and informed the DI to that effect. That evening when the day's routine was over (which included getting vaccinations in both arms), we were called out as a platoon and did physical drill under arms. The drill consisted primarily of "up and on shoulders," which was performed with our rifles, and they ran us through it about as long as we could stand it. That was penance for "some stupid motherfucker leaving wet socks in his bucket." It was pretty rough.

I had heard how the other marines would work over anyone who "fucked up" and caused the platoon to suffer. I expected to take a real hazing for my innocent mistake, but to my amazement not one man said even a word to condemn me. I guess they thought it was a little too much to expect me to anticipate that the lieutenant wouldn't want to see clean, wet socks in the bucket. I developed an increased respect and appreciation for my fellow "shitheads."

The first letter I wrote home after arriving in Dago was dated January 8, 1943.

> Dearest Mom and Dad,
>
> Haven't had a minute until now. Sorry but its that way. I took my shots today, got my uniforms (greens and stuff, no dress issue) and had my hair cut so short you might call it a shave. I am having a big time so far. I bunk with two of the boys from Denver. Good boys. I can see now why the Marines are so tough. Our sergeant is really tough but he knows his stuff to a "T." I have to hurry everything.
>
> We have had very little drill up until now. I imagine it will start soon. The eats are good, Mom. Dad, I haven't had time to concentrate on our little telegraphy deal[4] but maybe sometime. I'll write when I have time.
>
> Jim

There was little time for anything personal, including writing letters, but it was all just a blast to me, a light-hearted adventure. I enjoyed many rewards during the rigors of boot camp. There was a sincere satisfaction in being a contributing part of the growing "machine." It was thrilling to march with the other marines as we grew proficient in drill, especially when the band was there. The burn in your legs and lungs after you had marched all day had a good feeling to it. The Marine Corps seemed like a wonderful outfit. Until I got sick, that is. After that, it wasn't fun anymore. I had developed a severe case of what we called cat fever. I have no idea what it actually was, some sort of viral or bacterial infection, I suppose. There was quite a lot of it in camp.

I wanted so badly to graduate from boot camp with my platoon that I stayed on duty when I was so sick I should have gone to the hospital. The sensible thing to do was go to sick bay, turn in to the hospital, where you could get some medicine, and stay on a decent dry routine until you healed up a little. However, if you did that, you would be dropped from your platoon and then have to start over with a new outfit when you got out of the hospital. Because of my strong affinity to the guys in my platoon, I stayed there and marched in the rain with a high fever, a hell of a headache, and my nose running like a water fountain.

I had been picked as one of nine men from several hundred applicants to have a series of interviews for eventual field commissioned rank. As luck would have it, when I went for the last interview, with a captain, I was very sick. In full greens, sweating like a Russian wrestler, I went into the captain's office to be interviewed. It was very warm in the office, as it had been in the anteroom where I had been seated for some time, waiting my turn. The two handkerchiefs in my pockets were so full of snot that they showed wet on the outside of my greens. I had only been in the captain's office a few minutes when I got so woozy I had to fight to keep from passing out. The sweat was rolling off me and, naturally, my interview stunk. All the officers who had interviewed me previously, colonels and majors, recommended me for commission, but the captain did not. I was terribly dejected because I was the only one of the nine who wasn't advanced. I later tried to get the captain to grant me another hearing, after I felt better, but he would not.

So I learned firsthand what it is like to be a private in a marine line company, during a world war, for an extended period of time. I learned what it is like to be last in line to receive any available creature comforts and first in line to enter the maelstrom of battle. I learned firsthand of the criminal sickness that is war and of the terrible, unimaginable human behavior that is found there.

I lost my naive enthusiasm by virtue of this episode, and it put me on the bias with the corps. No matter how hard I tried, it seemed I couldn't get back on track. For a while I almost quit trying. It was over a year later, in the midst of a tough campaign, before I began to feel that I was back on top of it all. I believed by then that I could remain that way, if I could just live through it.

Anyway, toward the end of boot camp, I finally wore out the cat fever without leaving full duty, and I finished recruit training with the same bunch of men with whom I had started.

During those weeks I had written fifteen letters home. They are mostly very repetitive and very short. A typical letter was one page and would inform the folks of the status of the mail I was receiving, state some routine duties of the day, and ask them to send anything in short supply for us, especially candy of about any variety. I had never before cared particularly for sweets of any kind, including candy, cake, or the like. In boot camp, where no pogeybait (candy or other sweet edibles) was available for several weeks, thoughts of sweets became almost obsessive.

I had not expected Dago to get as cold as it did at night. Our little compo-board huts had no heat in them at all. We didn't have enough bedding to keep warm, and for a few nights I would wake up because of the cold. Soon I learned to wait until the night inspector had made his rounds, then I would get my overcoat out of my sea bag and spread it over myself like a comforter. That took care of that. I always got up before reveille anyway, so I would fold the overcoat and put it back in the sea bag before anyone noticed it.

One letter from me was quite a lot longer than the rest. It was written before I got so sick. The envelope is postmarked January 18, 1943, and the letter reads in part:

Dearest Mom and Dad,

Well, this is Sunday. The last two days we have had quite a little free time.

I went to Catholic church with a buddy of mine this morning. [That was Bob Stamm.]

We have more shots tomorrow. They are really corkers. We will start to work hard again Monday but I'll try to write if I have time.

Jim

Shortly thereafter came the fever and the fiasco of my final interview. After I was denied a commission, I was returned to duty under the old salts who had advanced in rank by their tenure in the corps. In the ranks of NCOs more than among the commissioned officers, there were many men who had joined the corps in peacetime, primarily to make a living. (NCOs — also called noncoms — were noncommissioned officers, corporals and sergeants.) When the war came along, they were promoted in rank more because of the expansion of the wartime corps than for their qualities of leadership. Many of them were patently envious of the status the new recruits had held in civilian life and were apprehensive of the recruits' potential to rise above them. If you happened to make the shitlist of one of these old salts, your very life could become precarious, and it would most certainly become unpleasant.

Though I had to deal with some troublesome NCOs, I was fortunate indeed in having two or three exceptional sergeants who were not of that ilk. I met one of them shortly after basic training and was associated with him for a long time. His name was Leon Utter, and in the course of more than two years we became close friends, like brothers.

Leon was from Miami, Oklahoma. His dad had been a marine, and Leon's life was steeped in the ritual of the corps — the esprit de corps. He wasn't very tall but was strongly built, and he always stood "chest out, chin in." He had military creases in his dungarees and he was often spotless, always as clean as possible under the prevailing conditions. His honesty, decency, and fairness were almost the sole cause of the return of my spirit and of my rededication to our high moral purpose.

At Dago, it was part of the procedure that the large number of men necessary to take care of the feeding of the boots (new recruits) would be furnished by some of the men who had just finished recruit training.

Most of the platoons, after finishing boot camp, would go on to rifle range and advanced training of one kind or another. A few unlucky platoons, of which mine was one, caught mess duty. When we graduated boot camp and became marines, we picked up our gear and carried it to a different part of the recruit depot. Our schedule there was physically very demanding.

We got up at 4 A.M. and dressed in white pants and T-shirt. Completing our attire was a white, knee-length bib-apron tied at the back of the neck and around the waist. This outfit was not nearly enough clothes to keep warm at 4 A.M. We marched to the mess hall around 4:30 and began preparation for the first stampede of boots coming in for morning chow. Each man had certain assigned duties. With Golightly, a good friend from Texas, I drew duty as a table jockey. Each jockey served seven tables and each table seated twelve men.

Early chow began around 5:30 A.M. and late morning chow ended around eight o'clock. When the last boot was out, the place looked like a shitstorm had hit it. It was our responsibility to clean the place. We cleaned it after every meal: morning, noon, and night.

The morning shift, however, was special. Between nine and ten o'clock, a captain wearing white gloves would inspect the hall. Our mess halls had exposed rafters. At times, the captain would stand on one of the tables and run his gloved hand down the top of the length of one or more of the rafters. At others, he would run it across the window sills, or even the deck. If his glove showed evidence of dirt, we would have a "field day" that night after evening chow. This consisted of hosing down the entire hall from the top of the roof crown to the floor and rubbing every inch of it dry. When we were done, the NCOs would inspect it. If it suited them, we could go back to our huts to take care of our personal hygiene, wash our clothes and gear, and get what sleep we could. The next morning, duty would begin again at 4 A.M. A stint of mess duty at that station lasted thirty days.

Any military organization has a certain number of fuck-offs, lazy and unconscionable duty dodgers who try to fake their way into no-duty status to avoid an unpleasant routine. And in any military organization, sick bay was generally the first place the fuck-offs would look to to accomplish such.

In the corps there were many duties that, though unpleasant, had their own reward in the satisfaction of doing a nasty job well. Mess duty, however, was both unpleasant *and* unrewarding. Sick call would furnish such an obvious chance for relief that the sick bay personnel were plainly skeptical of anyone on mess duty who made sick call.

If you were a table jockey, sick call took place at the same time you were serving chow to several hundred recruits. If you went to sick call, your fellow-jockey had to take care of your seven tables, along with his own, until you got back. It was a helluva bind to be in.

About two weeks into the mess duty, I began to feel lousy again. I thought perhaps my cat fever was recurring, but this bout was worse. For about a week I worked when I was so fatigued I had to drive myself to do the most common of activities. I had a headache all the time and a worsening rash of what I thought was prickly heat around my belly. I didn't go to sick call because I wasn't going to let Golightly down if I could help it.

One morning he said to me, "Johnston, you look like hell. Go see a doctor. I can take care of the fuckin' boots 'til you get back."

So I went to sick call, dressed in my white outfit that told everyone I was on mess duty. There I stood before two navy doctors. One of them looked at me, then turned to the other and said, "Look at this guy's posture. He needs to go back through boot camp again." To me the doctor said, "You'll be all right when you get off mess duty." He turned to the corpsman behind the counter and said, "Give this guy a couple of APCs." (An APC was a painkiller, like aspirin.) Then he left.

I didn't wait for the APCs. I took off back to the hall to help Golightly.

We weren't allowed freedom of the base, but that afternoon after we had finished the noon hall cleanup, I felt so bad that I put on my greens and took off to see if I could find someone who would help me. My bones all hurt, especially the joints, and my head throbbed miserably. I took off without direction into the area where the permanent personnel on the base were located, walking aimlessly, without knowing where I was going.

By the grace of God, who I am sure guided my footsteps, I came upon a beautifully kept area. There were yards of green grass and permanent buildings. I do not know the significance of the area or its primary purpose. On one of the building doors there was a little metal sign that said INFIRMARY.

I figured I had nothing to lose. I might walk into some place where I definitely was not supposed to be, but I felt so sick I thought I'd probably die anyway. Unannounced, I boldly opened the door and entered a fairly large room, occupied by one navy enlisted man sitting behind a desk. He had more stripes than I could recognize at the time. He looked up as I entered and said, "Yes, what is it, marine?"

For a moment I felt fear. What would they do to me? I was breaking rules. Then I thought, "What the hell. Do what you will."

To the sailor I said, "I'm sick, mate. I'm on mess duty at the recruit depot and it's hard work, but I'm not lazy. I don't mind hard work. I like it if I feel decent, but I'm sick — really sick."

He asked me if I had been to my own outfit's sick call and I told him, "I went to sick call this morning, but they didn't even examine me. Something is bad wrong, and if I don't get help I'm not going to make it."

The sailor looked closely at me and I could tell he believed me. He said, "I'll see what I can do."

He made a telephone call and when he had finished, he turned to me and said, "The doctor will come take a look at you."

In just a few minutes the door in the back of the room opened and in came a large, rather heavy-set, navy full lieutenant.

There wasn't any ceremony between the sailor and the doctor. They exchanged pleasantries and went about their business, showing no military convention at all.

I stood up at attention when the doctor came over to me, and he said, "Sit down, marine."

Then he said, "You're not feeling too good, huh? Let me see your tongue." He put his hand on my throat.

I opened my mouth and stuck out my tongue. He turned my head, first to one side and then the other. Then he said, "Well, son, you've got the measles. It's no wonder you feel bad. We better get you to the hospital," and they did so.

They must have notified my outfit because the next morning Golightly came to the hospital, bringing my gear. He didn't stay long. He had to get back to the tables. That was the last time I ever saw him. By the time I got out of the hospital, our mess duty was over and Golightly and the others had gone on to new assignments. I had gotten very debilitated (my hearing was particularly affected), and it took me quite a while to recuperate.

I have thought of the sailor and his doctor thousands of times through the years and always wished, as I do now, that in some way I could let them know what they mean to me. I don't know if you could die from measles, but I certainly feel that without their help, I would have died.

I later saw disease kill a marine on New Britain. The poor kid began to have patches of a skin fungus we called jungle rot. It got progressively worse. Before long, it nearly covered his entire body. He stunk badly. He should have been removed from that hot, humid, infectious environment, but he wasn't. Either from ignorance or indifference, he was kept there. The poison from the crud so permeated his system that he died.

To have a decent go of it in the corps, you had to be lucky, and in this instance my luck took a turn for the good.

When I got over the measles, I went back to duty. I was assigned to a training unit and moved to the rifle range at Camp Mathews, near Dago. There we began the days of snapping in — dry-firing our rifles, without ammunition — in preparation for firing with live ammo on the rifle range, for qualification as riflemen. It was fun.

Almost everything we did had a commonsense purpose: all the safety drills and precautions, the times we fired so as to zero in our weapons, the fires we built to boil water to scrub out the corrosive primer residue from our rifle bores, and finally the challenge of Record Day. On that day we fired a full course to earn the score that would be entered in our record books. We could see how well we had learned the lessons of marksmanship that the marine coaches taught so efficiently.

I had a superb rifle and two exceptional coaches. The coaches helped me set the sights on the rifle and zero in the piece, and when that was done the rifle just about did the rest. I was gratified to qualify as expert rifleman, the top of the three qualifying classifications for marine riflemen: marksman, sharpshooter, and expert.

It was the Marine Corps's intention that every marine, regardless of his job, be a qualified rifleman. Because the corps regarded competence with the rifle to be of the utmost importance, it authorized a special insignia to be worn if a marine scored high enough on the range to qualify as expert.

I remember as a boy reading in the old Lincoln Library book at home about the German casualties in the trenches in France. A high percentage of them that were opposite American positions were shot in the head. I wondered if I would ever be in a position to use my skill with the rifle, and I worried about what my reaction would be if I ever had a human being's head in my sights.

The rest of the time I spent in the States was uneventful for us marines. Following rifle training, we moved to Camp Elliot, an advanced infantry training base in the desolate hills inland from Dago. When the folks learned I would ship out before long, Dad somehow scrounged enough gasoline coupons so that he and Mother could drive out to see me. I was overjoyed. We had several wonderful hours together. I could generally get out of Camp Elliot on the few weekends left. Even on some weekday evenings, the folks could come out to the base reception center, where I could visit with them until taps, around ten o'clock. On the day we were to debark, we were restricted to the base in preparation, and the actual time we were to leave was naturally kept secret. One night I didn't show at the center, and the folks knew I was gone.

After I got home from the war, Mother told me that night at Camp Elliot was one of the saddest times of her life, almost like when my brother was killed. She said she and Dad had waited at the center and watched for me, looking down the road that I had always walked to get there. They waited until taps. When the base began to close down for the night, they knew they wouldn't be seeing me again, maybe for a long time, maybe never. Then they drove back to the little cabin they had rented near Dago and packed their things. Early next morning they paid Mr. Bailey, a transplanted Nebraskan who had rented them the cabin, and started the long thirty-five-mile-per-hour trip back to Nebraska.

After I had children of my own, I realized how much tougher that period of time was on the folks than it was on me. For me, though it was sad to part from the folks and a bit overwhelming to leave all the civilized things I was used to, I truly thought I was embarking on a great adventure.

I had considered well the very real possibility of dying before I got home again. Still, it would be a few weeks before I would begin to learn the many tortuous details that would accompany our promiscuous exposure to imminent death.

2. On to Australia

DURING THE WEEKS it took us to ship across when we left the States, I didn't write any letters. For those weeks, plus the time the folks were in Dago, there is a void in the continuity of the letters Mother saved. I have to concentrate much harder to remember that time as clearly as I do the times when I wrote with some regularity and have the letters to use for reference.

Those in charge at Camp Elliot in Dago assigned me to one of the little compo-board huts of the casual area. There was an unmistakable atmosphere around what the marines called a casual area. Having once been in one, you could always recognize them. It was obvious that there was nothing permanent there. No one would be there long. There were no footlockers, not even orange crates in which to store gear. There were no nameplates or unit designation stamps anywhere. Whatever was there would soon be gone. When you found yourself in a casual area (or a casual company), you knew for certain that you would soon be moving on.

I knew I was on my way to the South Pacific, which was fine. That is why I had joined the marines. That is why, when most of the men in my boot platoon had noted their preference for the aviation branch of the Marine Corps and had been granted that duty, I had entered my choice of duty as the Fleet Marine Force. But even though the routine was what I expected, when we moved from our training huts to the casual area, I had the uncanny feeling that I was to grow used to in the corps: the feeling that I was leaving home. Later in my tour of duty we moved out so often and so quickly that I would feel the same depressing emotion when we pulled out of a foxhole position where I had lived for only a couple of days.

Traveling the earth can sometimes be pleasant and it is often impressive. We boarded the big old green buses at the casual area and made the trip to the dock. When we unloaded I looked out over the ocean with an otherworldly feeling, "What is out there?" I took a long look west and thought, "How big is it?"

The ship against the dock would take me to where I would begin such a huge change in my life. A set of metal steps led up to the deck. It was odd to me that the water was deep enough to float a ship of that size right next to land. The ship looked large at the docks, but for an ocean-going vessel it was comparatively small. The Mormac Lines named some of their ships after birds. This one was the *Mormac Wren*. It was typical of the many Liberty ships built at that time to transport troops and cargo.

We sailed alone. No company. No escort. When we had been out a couple of weeks and there was nothing but water in every direction as far as the eye could see, the ship that had seemed so large when I boarded it began to seem very small.

Several days out, we ran into a storm. In the fierce winds and huge swells of the sea, the little *Mormac Wren* seemed even smaller. In the rough sea the propellers would come out of the water and turn faster than they were supposed to, and the little ship would shudder and vibrate.

I was fortunate in never being seasick. I did, however, feel queasiness enough at times to know about seasickness and so feel sorry for those affected by it. What bothered me most, as far as comfort was concerned, was the long periods of time with no freshwater baths. Saltwater showers always left me feeling sticky.

Troop rations on merchant marine ships, at least the ones I was on, were always short. I don't know if it is true or not, but we heard that the merchant cooks bid for the job of furnishing chow on troop ships. The lower their bid, the better was their chance of getting the job. For this reason troop chow was often less than bountiful. Noon chow was a bologna sandwich and an orange. It was adequate for survival, but we were always hungry — the ones who weren't seasick, that is.

There was an unusual lack of activity aboard ship that was lazy and pleasant for a while but that soon became very boring. We did learn the operation of the ship's guns and stood standby watch as auxiliary crews. It was an interesting break in the monotony.

We had been aboard ship about thirty days when I heard rumors we were heading for Australia. No one in the troops ever knew anything for certain until it was over, and even then there were generally questions. But, assuming some chance of fact in the scuttlebutt, I volunteered for guard watch topside on the *Mormac Wren* at about the time I thought we should be making our destination. I hoped I might thus sight land or shore lights when they first came into view.

The mass of marines aboard transport vessels was treated pretty much like livestock. Quarters were extremely cramped, and only the guard watch and certain small details had deck duty. Everyone else was below deck, where you couldn't see shit. I had luckily picked the right time to volunteer for guard duty and I was on watch when the first light was sighted. It was thrilling. I watched as slowly, ever so slowly, evidence of the mainland came into view. Before too long, I could make out other ships anchored in the harbor. A small pilot vessel came out to meet us. It took some time for us to reach the docks, and it seemed to me we were going to sail right into the city itself. It was Melbourne.

As far as I could see inland, in every direction, there were buildings and people. The buildings were different from any I had seen, the cars were different — nothing was the same, not even the names of the businesses. A bar was a pub; a drugstore, an apothecary. To a boy from a small Nebraska town on the plains, it was like a new world.

After endlessly stutter-fucking around getting ready, which was standard procedure for doing anything in the corps, we finally disembarked.

After that first long voyage on the ocean, when I stepped ashore the solid earth felt strange; almost as strange as the rolling deck of the ship had felt when we first put out to sea.

We boarded at a railway station for the forty- or fifty-mile trip inland to Camp Balcolm, the converted Australian women's army corps camp that served as the U.S. Marine base at Frankston, Australia.

The train was a very fast, efficient unit that the Aussies called a tram. It was somewhat like our interurbans, and I was told it traveled at speeds up to ninety miles per hour. Because some of the stations on its route were on one side of the tracks and some on the other, the tram had doorways on both sides. Station platforms were built up to the same height as the tram floor. When the tram stopped at a station, a small, wooden runway was lowered to cross the space between the tram and the platform for loading and unloading passengers. Many times the doors on the tram were left open and a small chain was snapped in place across the doorway to keep people from falling out.

As we started through Melbourne, I saw a strange site from the window overlooking the city. Hundreds of houses, covering miles on each side of the train tracks, had no shingles on the roofs. They were covered instead with rows of curved red tiles that looked like they were made of clay, somewhat like the old sewer tile that was still in use at that time in some places in the States. I wondered what would happen to the tiles if Melbourne ever had a good old Nebraska hailstorm.

We stopped a few times on our way to our destination and were allowed to mingle, in a very controlled way, with people at the places we stopped. Among the people were other U.S. Marines who were on liberty. A few times, timidly, we tried to strike up a conversation with some of their number, most of whom wore a royal-blue, diamond-shaped patch on the left sleeve. Arrayed on the blue diamond were five white stars in the pattern of the Southern Cross constellation. Down the middle of the diamond ran a big red numeral one, and stacked vertically from top to bottom of the numeral were white letters spelling GUA-DALCANAL. We were very cautious in our overtures, for we supposed they were all experienced in jungle war. Many of them were, but we soon learned that others were replacements who had gotten there only a few weeks before we did. None of them, however, seemed willing to spend any liberty time passing the word to a bunch of boot replacements.

We got off the tram at an open area where other U.S. Marines were on duty. They arranged us in ranks alphabetically and assigned us to units according to the first letters of our last names. They began to make assignments to the First Marines. I already had a great respect for the blue patch with the red numeral one on it and hoped I would draw that outfit. When the NCOs stopped assigning to the First Marines, I thought I had missed out, because I had erroneously assumed that the patch was the insignia of the First Marines. It was a few hours later that I learned the difference between the First Marines and the First Marine Division. The "First Marines" was in fact the First Marine *Regiment*, one of those in the First Marine Division, and the blue patch was a division insignia, not a regimental one. I was assigned to the Fifth Marines, another regiment of the First Division. When I found out what the Fifth was, I was grateful for the luck of the draw that made me part of that magnificent old regiment. At that time I didn't realize how many good men had paid, and would pay, with their lives to make the reputation and history of the Fifth. I had no idea what it would cost to be able to say I was part of E Company, Second Battalion, Fifth Marines. But I made up my mind that I would do my best to carry on the traditions of the Fifth, to honor former members and to pass on to those who would come later a heritage of which they could be proud.

All those guys who died can't tell you anything, so in their behalf, I'll try. I hope I'll be able to recount in an understandable way a little bit of why telling their story means so much to me. In so doing, I must constantly counsel myself not to contribute to a false image — a mistaken impression — of the glory and honor of the corps.

The glory and honor that are intrinsic parts of the corps stem from men having done what was required to complete dirty, difficult jobs successfully. The false image that I want to avoid, the one I would term the corps's glory bullshit, is the product of a public relations machine. It is designed for impressing the public and for recruiting, and it has very little to do with the real corps. It relies upon a number of gimmicks. I don't believe the corps is alone in this practice. The other armed services, I'm sure, also have their true glory and honor, apart from their glory show.

At that time there was a distinct difference in mental attitudes of Australians and Americans. In the States you could go most anywhere and never truly feel that there was a world conflict in progress. Not so in Australia. The Japanese got ominously close to that country. The Aussies were very aware of the danger, and it showed in almost everyone's demeanor.

On the way from Melbourne to Camp Balcolm the country was beautiful, rolling green hills and trees. Once in a while we could see a blacktop road winding through the hills. We stopped once, at a small town. We went into a little shop, or café, where we could buy tea if we had the right money, and we were allowed to do that. The attitude toward us new recruits was different than previously. Because of the immediate Japanese threat, the Australian civilian population seemed to hold us in higher regard than had U.S. civilians. More significant, the other men of the corps, those who had been in the Pacific Theater longer, looked upon us almost as individuals. We could plainly feel the difference, even though we were only lowly replacements, noncombatants.

Was this the same U.S. Marine Corps? Yes, it was the same corps, all right, and we would find out the reason for the change in attitude when we reached the South Pacific islands, as we were about to do. We would find that although the organization still had its distasteful side, an intense mutual respect of marine for marine was forged in the indelible experience of war.

Under the stress of battle, where true glory is born and grows, even the tradition of the corps was secondary to a man's respect for, and appreciation of, his comrades in arms. There was an intense respect for one another that grew greater among the front-line marines, the riflemen and machine gunners, as they became more experienced. Though a part of the corps's tradition, that mutual respect is not unique to the corps. I have heard the same emotion expressed by men who were not marines but who were in other infantry outfits, in a number of different wars. It is unique to those referred to as "trigger pullers," those who meet the enemy in close quarters. When you are up against it, really up against it, you don't fight for your country, or for the girl you left behind, or for apple pie. You fight for the guys sitting in the hole with you. Because you don't want to let them down, you do things you didn't believe you could make yourself do.

We arrived at Camp Balcolm, located in the hills near Frankston, a small town out in the boonies.[1] Upon arrival, a sergeant read off a list of names, one of them mine, and said, "Follow me." Our group was then led to our quarters and informed that we were assigned duty as machine gunners.

In the hut where I was quartered, I met the men of my unit, those that I would become so well acquainted with as the days passed. Our lives would depend on one another, subject to the will of God and the vagaries of chance, for as long as we lasted in the holocaust of war.

Among those men were some veterans of the long and miserable campaign on Tulagi and Guadalcanal and some new recruits, like me, who were replacements for the casualties of that campaign.

We immediately began the reorganization and training necessary to be ready for our next encounter. We spent much time in physical conditioning — calisthenics and hikes with battle equipment. We also put in an appreciable amount of time in the classroom studying the care and functioning of the equipment we would be using. Great emphasis was put on teaching the new men tactics we would use in the field and on characteristics and weapons of the Japs that the old guys had learned in previous battles.

While at Balcolm we were occasionally granted liberty. Most of the men spent that time in Melbourne, and a few took their leave in one of the small towns along the railway route between camp and the city.

During my long trip on the ship overseas, the folks grew anxious not hearing from me, so when I got to where I could, I sent some cablegrams. Rather than compose our own messages, we could pick from "canned" phrases that were provided. The one sent from Melbourne says

> received at 618 Dewey Street, North Platte, Nebr. 8HAC EFM
> IMP SANSORIGINE MARCORPS July 29, 1943. Mrs. Joshua T.
> Johnston, Wauneta, Nebr.
> Letters sent – my thoughts are with you – all my love.
> Jim Johnston 9 A.M.

I soon learned cables ordinarily took longer to get to the folks than air mail letters, so I quit sending the cables.

For a while all I had available was V-mail, the little one-page notes that were photographed smaller than they had been written. Typical was one written August 1.

> Dearest Mom and Dad,
>
> I just got back from liberty, which lasts 3 nights and days.
>
> I have a swell new buddy who is really good to me. He shows me the ropes. I am in the best, positively the most outstanding, unit of men in the world.
>
> I am content and happy. Your notes and the Bible are wonderful reading.
>
> I want you folks to stay happy and loving as you always were. Remember I am happy and am getting experience that gold can't buy.
>
> I send you my heart with each letter.
>
> Jim

My new buddy was Ted Himmelsbach, a short, dark-haired kid from Hershey, Pennsylvania. He was a magnificent person, brave, kind, and patient. Ted taught me all there was to know about the machine guns we used, which was a considerable amount of knowledge. When he had finished with me, I could literally take them apart and reassemble them blindfolded.

Ted was a gunner in a machine-gun squad who had come through Guadalcanal. His nickname was Snatch, pinned on him as a teasing allusion to his remarkably long manhood. (This, by the way, was characteristic of nicknames in the corps. Not always, but often, marines would seek out a man's most prominent physical feature, whether it was flattering or unflattering, and tag a nickname to him having to do with that feature.) Snatch and Cicero D. Moise, an easygoing Carolina boy that everybody called Mo, took me under their wings. In almost every way they were as different as left and right, night and day. Snatch was urbane and suave. He loved opera and he knew a great deal about it. Though his voice wasn't good, he often sang different parts of operas to me. He was especially fond of Pagliacci. Mo was a country boy, corny and unrefined. He sang, "A man came along / made me hush my song / threw me off a way out there."

But they both had shy, little-boy smiles and their hearts were big as washtubs. At the time I wondered why it was that those combat vets would have any concern for this noncombatant replacement. It was the beginning of my understanding of the brotherhood of the corps. They were trying to take care of me because I was a marine. They each took me to town to meet their girls. With Mo it was fun — a party, nothing serious. With Himmelsbach it was very serious — and sad. His friend was a beautiful black-haired girl. He loved her very much, but she didn't love him. She went places with him, but only as a harmless diversion. He was a friend to her, but no lover.

After we left Australia he would write her whenever he had the chance, far more often than he did his folks. On rare occasions he would hear from her, but she never led him on at all. It was just as well she never loved him. I imagine it saved her a lot of sadness and disappointment.

One letter that I wrote from Australia still comforts me. It is dated September 9, postmarked September 14, 1943.

> Dearest Mom and Dad,
>
> I am hearing from you in good order now. Your mail is coming through fine. Every letter I get from you folks is precious.
>
> I surely enjoy all the news you send me. You would be surprised how interesting the little things at home are. You two are with me always.
>
> Isn't love a power? Mighty blasts cannot shake it; hate cannot conquer it; money cannot buy it. It knows no bounds, or even modifications. It spans oceans as easily as we walk across the room — and death only makes it stronger.
>
> I'm especially happy this evening. I guess the best way to explain it is the way Dad did once long ago — "It's a big book."
>
> Jim

I was so grateful then, and I am so thankful now, that I didn't get killed before I had a chance to tell the folks how I felt in my heart for them.

When I was given liberty the first time, I made the trip to Melbourne. I went into a pub with some of the boys and drank what the Aussies called "nose knockers," mainly because I felt it was expected of me.

To make a nose knocker, you set a shot glass in a beer mug and poured it full of scotch whiskey. Then you filled the mug with 12 percent beer. When you finished drinking the mixture, the shot glass would slide down the mug and hit you on the nose.

While I was there I ran into a marine who had been a friend of mine in the States. He had been assigned to the First Regiment. They were stationed at the cricket grounds in Melbourne and had overnight liberty regularly. In the course of the evening, he asked me if I had gotten laid. I told him no and asked if he had. He answered, "Almost. I had a girl and she was ready, willing, and able, but I had gotten too far behind. I just got started and was finished." He chuckled a little and added, "She said 'C'mon Yank, give me a go.'" I guess the marines didn't *always* get the job done. Anyway, I ended up drinking too many nose knockers and came in early, dizzy and disoriented.

Another night when our outfit had liberty, I decided to go to town with Nesbitt, a buddy from my unit. We bought two cartons of cigarettes for fifty cents a carton, tax-free, at the PX (post exchange, the enlisted man's general store), and went to Melbourne.

We went to Flinders Street Station in the city, which I was told was the largest railway station in the world. I don't know if that was so, but I do know it was huge. We just stood around, holding our cartons of cigarettes, and watched the people. It was fun. It wasn't long before an Aussie came by and traded us two fifths of King's Court scotch for the cigarettes.

We were issued blouses we called Eisenhower jackets to wear in Australia. They were short wool jackets, very full and loose in the upper part but buttoned tight around the waist. You could carry a fifth of liquor in the jacket without much showing, but you needed to make sure the bottom was buttoned.

I slipped one fifth in my jacket in good shape, but Nesbitt forgot the buttons on his blouse. When he put his fifth in his jacket it slipped right on through and busted on the station's concrete floor. He looked at me and said, "What are we gonna do now?"

I said, "Nesbitt, I don't know what you're gonna do, but one bottle isn't enough for four people to party on."

He knew I was right, so he took off for somewhere and I went looking for a Sheila. (Sheila was Australian slang for a young woman, a gal.) In the course of the afternoon, I saw a likely prospect and asked her if she would like to get something to eat. We went to some kind of a café and got some chow. By the time we had finished eating, it was pretty obvious that we didn't fit. As kindly as I could I said, "Lady, I don't think this is going to work."

She smiled and answered, "You're right, marine," and went on her way.

I went back to the barracks early again with my King's Court. As opportunities presented themselves, Himmelsbach and I eventually finished it off.

I only had a couple of chances for liberty after I went to Melbourne with Nesbitt. I would find a clean eating-house, get me a good breakfast of steak and eggs, then go back to the Red Cross building to read or occupy myself some other way until sack time. Then I'd crawl into one of their stacked bunks (because it was the cheapest place to stay) and sleep until daylight. You had to sleep on or in your clothes and shoes, or someone would steal them while you slept. I was grateful for liberty for the respite it afforded from the military routine, but it wasn't party time for me. I was afraid to drink enough booze to get forgetful, fearing what might happen to me in a strange country. And the specter of venereal disease was a serious deterrent, for me. Marines were screwing Aussie girls all over the place, sometimes mothers and daughters in the same sack, but it wasn't worth the risk. I had seen so many marines stand sweating in pain at the urinal that I couldn't work up any passion over the Aussie girls.

As an example I cite one Bad Eye Smith (so called because of a drooping eyelid). He had a girlfriend but he couldn't make her, and he informed us all that he had found a virgin among the Aussie gals. After he did eventually score with her, he said she told him she had broken her maidenhead riding a horse. She must have gotten stuck on a diseased saddlehorn because Bad Eye came down with a particularly nettlesome strain of veneral disease commonly known among the troops as Egyptian clap.

One morning I was sitting in the anteroom of the Red Cross waiting for transportation back to Balcolm. My liberty wasn't up, but I just wasn't interested in the rat race. One of the guys sitting beside me nudged me and nodded at a big marine standing in the room. He said, "That's John Gibson. He's over the hill."

Gibson was from Paris, Tennessee. He was big, strong as an ox, and tougher than boot leather. I had heard some of the old guys talk about him before, but that was the first time I had ever seen him. He had been AWOL for some time. In a little while he ambled over near us. The man sitting beside me asked him, "Are you turning in, Gibson?"

He answered that he was. He said he was broke. I asked him if that was the only reason he was going in, and he said it was. I still had a few pounds over the cost of fare back to camp, and I asked Gibson if he would want it. He was a little flabbergasted, you could tell, but when I proffered the pound notes to him he accepted them quickly and took off around the corner of the building.

That was the last I saw of John until we were about ready to shove off for New Guinea. I was satisfied I had seen the last of the pounds. As a matter of fact, that's what I thought when I gave them to him. I didn't expect ever to get them back, but I was to learn different about Gibson as the days went by. He was a good, conscientious person and had been a hell of a marine — a corporal. Unfortunately, Gibson's allegiance to the corps had been alienated.

The division had come off Guadalcanal in bad shape, lots of malaria and jaundice, along with other infirmities. A colonel decided he was going to whip the outfit into shape, and he started by putting Gibson's unit into a seventy-five-mile forced march. Gibson was a machine gun squad leader. They carried their heavy guns on the march. When the gunner in Gibson's squad faltered under the weight of the tripod used to support the heavy gun, Gibson took it himself. He carried it until he became disgusted with the futility of the exercise, and then he dumped the big pod in the ditch. When the march was over, he went back for the pod but it was gone. They gave John a pretty heavy court martial, broke him in rank, made him pay several hundred dollars for the pod, and completely destroyed any tolerance he had for the shortcomings of the corps.

Gibson and I would later become fast friends. He was a little reckless, and I guess it kind of rubbed off on me. We played catch with hand grenades. We also played a game of throwing knives at one another's feet. We would stand facing one another, two or three steps apart. One of us would extend one foot on the ground in front of the other man, who would throw his knife to stick into the ground as close as possible to the first man's foot *without hitting it*. Then there would be a turnabout, with the first knife thrower putting his foot in front of the other man, who would take his turn as thrower. Whoever threw his knife closest to the other man's foot won the contest. The knife had to stand upright to count. If you moved your foot, you lost. If you hit the other man's foot, you lost.

I still have a tattooed spot on the lobe of my left ear where the point of Gibson's fountain pen struck in another of our games. Our games were admittedly a little rough, but they didn't seem so wild then. Those were pretty rough times.

John paid me back every cent of the money I gave him in Melbourne. He was brave and loyal. He'd have died before he'd have left a buddy in a tight spot in combat. He would do about anything to escape the corps's petty elements, but he was always ready when it came time to go to war. In the bush and in the war he was as good a man as I ever knew, but when the fighting was over, as far as Gibson was concerned the chain of command could go fuck itself.

At Camp Balcolm one of my NCOs, Hook Peletier, taught me the care, handling, and use of the .45 pistol. (Peletier told his girlfriend he got his nickname from the extraordinary curve ball he could throw. In actual fact, the name came from his prominent, arching nose.)

Peletier also explained the procedure of being a prisoner "chaser" (meaning an escort) and told me it was policy that if you let a prisoner escape, you served his sentence. One morning I was issued a .45 and cartridge belt and directed to an area where I was to take charge of a prisoner and chase him to the brig. There, I was to turn him over to the NCO in charge. I was very apprehensive about the responsibility placed on me. When I got to the designated pickup area, I was also disappointed and embarrassed. The man I was to guard was a marine known as Big Tom, one of the few remaining China marines.[2] As we left the area I said to him, "Sir, I am very sorry I was given this duty. I have no right to be taking you anywhere."

Big Tom turned his head to me and smiled. "It's not up to you, lad. Don't let it bother you. Let's be on with it."

So I took him on to the brig and left him there to serve three days' solitary on piss and punk (bread and water) for missing the last tram that ran at midnight from Melbourne back to Frankston.

That evening there was another disheartening incident. When the day's routine was over and most of us were getting ready for evening chow, Himmelsbach was hard at work building an HMO — a heavy marching order. It consisted of two full packs (a knapsack and haversack) hooked together, with a bedroll of blanket and poncho wrapped around them and with entrenching tool attached. When the rest of us went to chow, Snatch was out on the parade ground in full uniform, leggings and all, cartridge belt, weapon, helmet and HMO, marching all alone, around and around. After we came back from chow, even after the sun went down (and I don't know how much longer), Snatch was still out there, going around and around. He finally came back into the barracks. He must have been out there several hours, at least. Everything on him was wet with sweat. I never did find out what he was paying for. He was the first man in our squad — that meant he was a top man — a good marine, but the corps did not discriminate when it came to meting out shit details as disciplinary action.

Personally, I can count at least 105 days I spent on shit detail. It was most all for letting someone know how I felt when I should have kept my mouth shut. One platoon sergeant, a good man and a credit to the corps, accounted for about sixty days of my punishment. I'll have to admit, though, it was probably my fault. In a rear area on New Guinea (our destination after leaving Camp Balcolm), I had shared a bottle of whiskey with a major, unbeknownst to the major.

It was quite a feat, actually, getting the bottle of whiskey. I sneaked into the major's tent in the dark of night and five-fingered it from under his sack. The tricky part was that the major was asleep in the sack. It's a wonder I wasn't caught red-handed. I was the only private in the First Division celebrating in the jungle in the wee small hours, though, so it wasn't too difficult to figure out who got the major's booze.

For that I drew thirty days' walloping pots and pans. They were big and greasy, and they had to be washed in boiling water. We boiled the water by building big wood fires under half-barrels full of water. We were only a few degrees latitude off the equator. Not very pleasant duty.

On the last day of the detail, I had just hung up the last big old steel pot when I said to a messmate, "Well, I hope Hollingsworth [the platoon sergeant] is satisfied." I could tell from the expression on my buddy's face that I had talked when I should have been listening. I turned around and saw Holly standing right behind me.

Holly said, "No, but thirty days on the garbage scow will satisfy me."

That meant loading oil drums full of greasy, stinking garbage from the whole regiment onto ten wheel trucks, hauling it down to the bay, loading it onto barges, towing it out in the drink, and dumping it out for the sharks. I didn't have to do the full thirty though. Before my time was up, we shoved off for the war.

Thinking back, whenever we weren't fighting the war I was damn near always on shit detail. Once in a while, though, I lucked out — for instance, when I caught duty on the detail that was sent to the back country of Australia to cut wood.

That effectively eliminated liberty. There were no three-day passes given, and less time just wouldn't do us any good. The detail was so far from town that the travel time in and back didn't leave a man any appreciable time in the city. Also, transportation schedules for that remote part of the country didn't coincide with our free time. So we cut firewood for the division's heating and cooking stoves from early morning 'til near sundown.

I was a trimmer, an axe man. We cut down the smaller trees, up to eight or ten inches in diameter, and trimmed the logs so the buzz saw crews could cut them up, stove-size. The captain in charge had a shack-

33

up job in town and I never saw him at the lumber camp. There were no inspections and the work felt good. I scrounged a file from some motor pool people so I could sharpen my axe. It was the best duty I ever had in the corps. An Aussie dairy truck came by in the early morning darkness and left bottles of fresh milk at the mess tent. The mess guards never stood their watch, so I'd get up before the cooks did and take a bottle of milk each morning for breakfast. When the cooks had emptied some of the other bottles, generally by noon chow, I would put my empty bottle back. That worked as long as the detail lasted.

There were a couple of Jewish boys there who entertained us every so often by playing tricks on one another. They were pretty outrageous jokes, often quite rough, but almost always fun to watch. One of the boys slept in the same tent with me, and the other somewhere else. One night after taps someone sneaked into our tent, armed with a bucket of water. It was the Jewish boy who slept elsewhere. He dumped it on his buddy in the sack and took off. You could hear them most of the rest of the night, ramming around chasing one another.

The wood chopping detail was fun but, as is sometimes the case, you have to pay later for the good times you are having. The last few days we were out there, the men on normal duty back at camp got one hypodermic vaccination each day for five days. The shots were preventive measures against a variety of maladies that awaited us in the jungle. When we came back to camp, I had just one day to get all the shots. So I went to the medical hut and got two shots in one arm, one in the other arm, and one in each cheek of my butt. It was hot in the hut and I was in full greens, including Eisenhower jacket. When I came out I was sweating profusely, and the world spun dizzily. I sat down on the steps of one of the adjacent huts, hoping I wouldn't pass out. I put my head between my knees and breathed deeply. Pretty soon the world stabilized. I stood up and walked gingerly back to my bunk in the company area. I started sorting my gear and loading up to get ready for the trip to eastern New Guinea.

We had a farewell party on the parade grounds at Camp Balcolm. Our company had been in Australia for a few weeks, and everyone knew we were going to war. There were kegs of beer set up along the edge of the company area. That bunch of marines saying goodbye to Australia and getting ready to go back to the disease and Jap-infested jungles put together a pretty wild party. One of the beer kegs kept running slow, even though it was half full. Someone finally busted the top out of the keg and found the carcass of a black snake plugging up the bung of the keg. There were several puking marines when they found out what they'd been drinking.

3. New Guinea and the Jungle

IT WAS A LONG, hot two-thousand-mile ocean voyage from our camp in Australia to the shores of New Guinea. Except for an occasional Condition Red and General Quarters, it was boring, and there were no freshwater baths. Sticky, sweaty, smelly. One thing that broke the monotony was sighting a group of whales that came near our ship. We watched them cavorting for several hours.

On the way to New Guinea, we dropped anchor in the bay at Townsville, Australia. It was very warm, but we weren't allowed to swim off the Liberty ship that was transporting us. George Hartley and I decided that I would fall off the fantail into the cool bay water, and he would jump in to save me. I eased my way back to the fantail railing and looked down into the water. There was a big fish — an ugly, queer looker — lazing along the top. I called Hartley, "Hey, George, c'mere and look at this."

He came back to the railing and when he saw the creature he said, "Oh shit! Don't fall in now. That's a hammerhead." He went on to explain that the hammerhead was a shark.

Hartley was a buddy of mine from Miami whose dad was an executive with one of the big airlines. George wasn't good-looking (in fact, I refrain from saying he was homely more out of respect for him than respect for the truth), but he had an abundance of self-confidence. He wasn't a big man, neither tall nor stocky, but he was very muscular. He could do flips and other gymnastic stunts, and he was adept at about any water sport (swimming, diving, and the like). He was an accomplished Ping-Pong player, and I never did beat him at checkers. He was quite a lot heavier than I, but I boxed with him anyway. One time, even with the heavily padded gloves we used, he cracked one of my ribs. Meaning it as a compliment, I would say Hartley was pretty much of a racketeer. He seemed to find out where the best available of everything was located, and to figure some way to take advantage of the good deals. To my good fortune, he was a true friend and was never reluctant to share whatever bounty he had with me.

One time on New Guinea, after a long, hard rain, I got caught in the current of a swollen stream. My hometown had a river running through it, and I had become a decent swimmer, but that time in New Guinea I was having a hell of a time trying to stay above water. I was in real danger of being swept away by the turbulent current. Without hesitation, Hartley jumped into that turmoil and lent his strength to bail me out. I have serious doubts that I could have made it without him.

As you can see, George was a good man to know, especially when you were close to the water.

When we finally got to New Guinea, it looked great from the ship, green and beautiful. We landed without incident at Milne Bay and spent the next few days setting up a temporary base from which we would conduct operations. We began the routine of our schedule, sending out company- and battalion-size patrols into the hills.

For the men of the First Marine Division, New Guinea was a cheap star in our campaign bar. The action to secure it had been an army show and there were no sizable Jap forces left when we arrived. We were there to keep an eye on the place and, primarily, to prepare for invasions farther north. In doing so, we learned about the hard work of jungle patrols.

What had appeared green and beautiful from the ship was pretty much an ugly mass when we got ashore. The terrain was rugged, with hills that were steep and high, covered with large boulders or muddy jungle. We made several combat patrols, fully loaded and prepared, that were physically tortuous. Wading against the torrents of mountain streams while carrying a load that was extremely awkward and heavy, we learned to look out for crocodiles and snakes. Mosquitoes were thick, as were leeches. There were bugs of many kinds, including the little black bastards with the forked tails that bent back up over their heads like scorpions. When they stung you it would hurt for hours.

Occasionally in our operations we would come across little groups of natives. They were very dark, bushy-haired people we called "fuzzie wuzzies." They were not openly hostile, but neither were they friendly. Their men carried big, machete-like knives, and I made it a point never to turn my back on one of them. I don't think they would have been averse to killing a marine for anything of value had they been given a chance to get away with it.

It was on New Guinea that I first heard the unique drone of the engines in the Jap Mitsubishi bombers, and first felt the distinct apprehension created by enemy aircraft overhead. It seemed odd to me that they could fly over us, unmolested, and they left me with a helpless feeling. They would drop their bombs and go on their way. We were fortunate to be far enough from the concentrated target areas that the bombs didn't fall among us. That would change, later in the war.

Our patrols would each last several days and nights. We would move during the daylight hours, and at night we would set up perimeter defenses to protect ourselves against any surprises. When a patrol was finished and we returned to our base camp, we were given some time off to clean our gear and write letters, or whatever else we could find to do.

After we left Australia, it was several days before I had any stationery except V-mail available. About all I ever wrote on V-mail was just a note to let the folks know I was still alive. The next real letter I wrote was on Red Cross stationery. There was a Red Cross tent on the army area beach on New Guinea, and once in a while our schedule was such that we could sneak off to the tent.

I'll have to admit I wasn't what you would call a wholehearted Red Cross fan. It always seemed to me that their female representatives catered too much to the brass, not that I could blame them. That is where the money and power were. If I had been one of them, I would probably have done the same. Anyway, I was happy to get a few sheets of their paper.

The first letter on Red Cross paper was written during the first three days of November and is postmarked with yet another date.

November 1, 1943

Dearest Mom and Dad,

It's been a couple days since I heard from you. I hear from some of the girls at home quite regularly.

It seems odd that you can't get helpers on the farm.

There is some talk of a two-dollar-a-day bonus for all the time you've spent in the service since the start of the war and two dollars and fifty cents for every day you spend overseas. Everyone here is jubilant even over the prospects of it.

Mother, I am making out a bond allotment to you for $37.50 per month. I don't know how long it will take to get it started, but it will probably be quite a while. It isn't very much, but at least I can feel like I'm contributing a little to the cause.

Well, I've rambled long enough, so I'd better give up for this time and try to do better the next.

Jim

The next letter is also on Red Cross paper.

Dearest Mom and Dad,

It has been 5 days since I wrote you last. I have been busy and I really mean busy. Dad, I heard one of my buddies sing a song that you and Mom would really have liked. It is named "Rozita." It is beautiful. It is about a fellow who loved a girl and serenaded her but she met another guy and the song is the first guy's lamentation. It is the music that is best, even though the sentiment is really touching.

I am getting your mail fine. Have gotten the cigarettes Alice[1] and [a girl] sent but no packages from you as yet. They will be along some of these days.

Did you know Lefty Egle is gone?[2] They really got him in a hurry didn't they? Sometimes when I think of things like that I get kinda blue, not because I'm afraid to die, but just because I wouldn't get to see you folks any more.

Then I think that, at best, a life is pretty short, and we'll all be together again before long on the other side.

I often look for the plan of life. It is rather difficult to look alone. That is really the way to find it, I guess, but it is disconcerting to argue with yourself. I miss our family discussions of philosophies of the metaphysical more than anything else.

I'm still so proud it hurts that I'm a Marine. I'm one of the Second Battalion Fifth.

Jim

In the days between those letters something happened that has probably afforded me more laughs than any other one thing in my life. It was anything but funny while it was taking place, but all through the years it has made me laugh every time I think of it.

In our off-duty time, we tried to familiarize ourselves with what New Guinea had to offer. Whenever we had a little time on our own, we would reconnoiter new ground, scavenging for anything useful we could lay our hands on. On this occasion Justin Kollman was with me and Hartley. Kollman was a big, strong man from Montana who reminded me of a tall, straight pine tree. He was a country boy, through and through, and lacked any of the city's sophistication (of which Hartley possessed so much). Justin was a genuinely nice guy, quiet and unassuming. He seldom said more than a few words, but he was always kind and helpful if you needed him.

So the three of us set out: Kollman, the naive; Hartley, the sharpy; and of course me, the misfit. During some of our training activities we had noticed huge army supply dumps in different areas, and our mission of this day was to find a dump where we could make a midnight requisition of something good to eat.

Along the area close to the beach, the army engineers had built some very good graded roads. Occasionally a narrow causeway had been built out from the main road into what was virtually swampland. At the end of the causeway we had chosen to investigate, there was a large platform constructed of coconut logs and stacked with many wooden boxes. The causeway was at least a hundred yards long and was totally exposed. There was no cover, nowhere to hide along it, so we waited until we thought we could make it all the way to the dump without being

New Guinea and the Jungle

seen. Once there, we could hide among the boxes while we checked them out for any kind of sweet chow.

We negotiated the entry in good order and were soon out of sight from the road. We began our search in earnest and in a short time met with great success: One part of the stacks was all canned food. Many cases contained only sweet potatoes or beets and such, but in the midst of the stacks Hartley found a case marked simply "Choice Pieces." Hartley pried the boards loose on the top of the case and to our great joy lifted out a shiny tin can with a bright blue label on which was printed "Dole Pineapple Choice Pieces." We knifed open one can and ate the sweet chunks. It was delicious. We were ecstatic: Here we had a whole case of cans of this wonderful tidbit. We decided to load up what we could reasonably carry and get away from there as quickly as possible, hoping to return at some later time. We loaded our pockets and stuffed cans inside our clothing — perhaps too many cans, because the shiny metal ends and the blue labels bulged conspicuously from the pockets of our dungarees. We waited until there was no traffic on the main road and then started hurriedly along the long, narrow causeway.

When we were about half-way along the causeway (our most ex-posed, vulnerable position), down the intersecting road came a jeep with three army officers in it, going like hell. Bad, bad luck! We slowed to a nonchalant walk, hoping that we wouldn't look out of place and that they would go by without noticing us. They went past the causeway all right, but not very far. The driver slammed on the brakes. The jeep slid to a stop on the road, turned around, came back to the causeway en-trance, turned in, and started down the narrow grade, straight at us.

We were caught! There was nowhere to go, no way out. No telling how deep the water was on both sides of the causeway, nor what was in the water. Besides, if we ran, the officers in the jeep would probably shoot us. They could have killed us in that situation without fear of retribution.

Kollman was nearest the jeep when it stopped in front of us. The offi-cers in it were a general, a colonel, and a captain. I did not know then, and I am not certain now, who the general was. He had more than one star and there were stars all over his jeep. During my entire tour of duty in the corps, as in all the years since, that is the only time I was that physically close to a general. He asked Kollman, "What are you boys doing?"

Kollman didn't answer.

"Did you hear the general, boy?" the captain shouted, very agitated. Kollman answered, "Yeah."

Hartley and I tried to shrink into nothing. Any chance we might have had to escape trouble by snapping to and brown-nosing the general, was gone. With Kollman as our spokesman, neither was there much chance of fabricating a slick excuse, the likes of which Hartley might have been able to come up with.

The captain was steaming. "Don't you know who this is?" he railed.

The general held up his hand to quiet the captain and spoke again to Kollman. "What have you got there, son?"

Kollman, in naive desperation, answered the general with one word: "Coconuts."

Now, you must understand that all around us were coconut trees, abundant in that part of the islands, and the coconuts themselves were everywhere underfoot, constantly in the way. One thing you certainly would not carry around was a coconut. Obviously, coconuts didn't have shiny metal tops and bright blue labels, either.

I began silently to hope that our punishment would not be too severe.

The captain began another tirade, and once again the general held up his hand. Miraculously, unbelievably, he was grinning. To the captain he said, "Let's go."

The captain, almost forgetting his station, was incredulous. "Sir?" he asked.

"I said, 'Let's go,'" the general answered.

The captain remembered his place. He quickly backed the jeep out and took off down the main road.

We three buddies got out of there as fast as we could. When we had gone far enough that we figured we were out of harm's way, we laid down by the side of the road and, in our relief, laughed until our bellies ached. We could have been in real trouble, and it is a wonder that we avoided it. We were in an ideal place to be made an example for the rest of the marines newly arrived on New Guinea.

There is no telling what prompted the general's reaction. Naturally, he had more important things to worry about. Or maybe he thought that sometime he might need a marine who wouldn't be there if he had been sent to the brig. Maybe the general thought back about the time when he was a young soldier, or maybe it was just that the utter absurdity of what Justin had said struck the general's funny bone.

At any rate we went back to our own territory with light hearts and, incidentally, several cans of "Choice Pieces."

Kollman was a real man and a good friend. He was a hell of a marine who died doing a hell of a job in a hell of a place. But whenever I think of him, I always remember "coconuts."

After those largely uneventful few weeks on New Guinea, we loaded our gear and headed for the war.

4. New Britain: My First Good Look at the Monkey Show

IN A LETTER to his sister written January 1, 1863, in Murfreesboro, Tennessee, Thomas Worley said of Civil War battle, "Martha, I can inform you that I have seen the monkey show at last, and I don't want to see it no more."

What a colorful expression that is. To the uninitiated, combat can appear to be what seemed a monkey show to a guileless, nineteenth-century American boy. Odd, fascinating, possessed of the exotic and the exciting, something akin to a circus. To those of experience, of course, war's horrific confusion is a different matter entirely. The irony in this expression of Thomas Worley's enlightenment is, to me, very moving.

The time was rapidly approaching when I would learn that among the thousands of men who served in World War II, most all of them good men, only a comparative few would see the "monkey show." Not many people have been front-line troops. There is a decided difference between that position and any other. Not many have charged or defended against hostile ground forces in strength, with no one between them and a determined enemy. This is especially true if you add the phrase "for a long period of time." In relation to the total number of armed forces, the number of front-line troops in World War II was very small, even at its peak. And the nature of their duty rapidly diminished their numbers ever further. Of those who had been left there a couple of years, not many remained.

The First Marine Division was formed as a division of infantry. In its entirety, it was a large, complex unit. It contained many people that are not commonly thought of as infantry: a regiment of engineers, a regiment of artillery, motor transport units, headquarters personnel, and other outfits that I am not familiar with.

The First Division contained three infantry regiments: the First, Fifth, and Seventh. In the army my regiment would have been known as the Fifth Infantry Regiment. In the corps it was called, simply, the Fifth Marines.

Our regiment was made up of three battalions: the First, Second, and Third. At the beginning of the war, each battalion contained three rifle companies, a weapons company, and a headquarters company. In battle, the machine gunners in the weapons company were attached to the various rifle companies. As the war progressed, demanding maximum, and immediately available firepower, the weapons companies were disbanded and the machine gunners were permanently transferred into the rifle companies. The 81MM mortar men and the rest of the weapons company were transferred to headquarters company.

In combat, each rifle company had three platoons, each consisting of three rifle squads and two machine-gun squads. These squads formed the front line of troops that faced flat-trajectory fire — fire from enemy machine-gun and rifle rounds. In addition, each rifle company had one platoon of 60MM mortars that was deployed several hundred yards behind the lines in defiladed areas.

The magnificent navy pharmacist's mates (called corpsmen) who cared for our casualties in battle were technically part of headquarters company. However, they were assigned to and went with the rifle companies to do their job.

As for the numbers, there were 175 or 180 riflemen and machine gunners in each company. There were three companies to a battalion, three battalions to a regiment, and three regiments to a division. Thus, close to 4,860 men took the brunt of the initial landings and fought eyeball-to-eyeball with the Japs. Those troops suffered the huge preponderance of the casualties in the division statistics.

Those of us among the flat-trajectory troops had many a good laugh out of the dubious solace to be found in not having to worry about getting transferred. Where could they send us that would be worse?

Even the mortarmen and artillerymen, whose jobs were very difficult in themselves, lived under the threat of transfer to the front-line troops. Those people who handled high-trajectory projectiles weren't actually in the same league with line troops. If they ever saw the enemy within rifle range, it was a highly unusual occasion. They had tough times aplenty, but nothing like the constant exposure to enemy flat-trajectory fire that was the daily and nightly fare of our riflemen and machine gunners.

The men of my original squad, and the men who were with that squad as replacements, suffered 300 percent casualties and a mortality rate above 83 percent. Twenty-seven men that I knew well were killed, including eight of my closest buddies who were killed by bullets from small arms or bayonets. I imagine that the mortality rate was quite typical for most squads of riflemen or machine gunners who were in the area two years or longer. The possible exception to that would be the "old men" who had fought only on Guadalcanal, Eastern New Guinea, and New Britain — the earlier campaigns of the war. They were there in the Pacific theater a long time and endured some of the most miserable of physical duties. They had many casualties, also, but nothing like the numbers in the later campaigns during which the machine guns were made permanently part of the line companies. I knew one squad in E Company that had, by the numbers, a 100 percent mortality rate. Like mine, it was a squad of machine gunners. They lost two-thirds of their unit in one assault.

I think we used our guns a little less sparingly, and kept them more quickly available in closer concert with the riflemen, than most infantry outfits, even those in the corps. Many times when we advanced we did so with two rifle squads in front of our machine gun section and one rifle squad behind it. As was later shown by the numbers of enemy we eliminated, it was a highly efficient use of the guns, even if it was costly in casualties.

From our last station on New Guinea, it was a little over three hundred miles northwest over Huon Gulf, through Vitiaz Strait and across Dampier Strait to the western tip of the island of New Britain. On the north side of that western tip was Cape Gloucester. At that time I had never heard of the place.

The old salts talked of many different Jap strongholds in the islands, one named Rabaul. It was located on the northeast part of New Britain, on the Gazelle Peninsula. At the time, no one confided in me what our mission was. We were to secure the airport at Cape Gloucester, make patrols inland through the jungled mountains, and make new landings up the island coast to hamper the effectiveness of the powerful forces that the Japs had based at Rabaul.

You can find a fairly accurate academic description of New Britain in about any good reference encyclopedia. The island is approximately three hundred miles long and averages about fifty miles wide. In that fifty miles of width, the land rises from sea level to more than 7,500 feet of elevation, then returns to sea level on the other side. (The highest elevation on the island is nearly half again as high as Denver, the "Mile High City.") New Britain has an equatorial climate with heavy rainfall, owing both to the mountains and to its position athwart both prevailing winds, the northwest monsoons (December–March) and the southeast trades (May–October). There are three areas of active volcanism. The capital of the Territory of New Guinea (of which New Britain was a part) was formerly located at Rabaul. After a volcanic eruption killed nearly three hundred people there in 1937, the capital was moved to Lae on the main island of New Guinea.

That is a fairly good textbook description of New Britain. Not a bad place, if you could live in a house by the beach. However, to fight a campaign there during the monsoon season, in some of the heaviest rainfall on earth, is a different proposition.

I do not understand why New Britain is seldom mentioned as a major campaign of World War II. Besides spending about four months in most unpleasant and trying conditions, the First Division suffered 1,327 battle casualties while successfully neutralizing sizable amounts of Jap territory and personnel. God alone knows how many more casualties resulted from accidents and the many maladies, both natural and unnatural, that were so common among newcomers to the area. I have been able to find very little written about the various landings and battles on New Britain. I doubt that I will be able to do them justice. I was so new to the corps and so low down in the organization — that I seldom got my head up far enough to know what was happening. I didn't even know the names of some of the guys in my own outfit that were blown to hell within my sight.

When it came time to move north to an impatiently waiting war, we made one leg of the journey on an Australian ship, the *Westralia*. It had a different feel, hard to explain, than the American ships I had ridden. Maybe the Aussie crew and their procedures made it seem foreign, but that wasn't all. The ship had a different shape, and the motors pounded differently. One real novelty to us was the screened-in square structures on the deck, enclosing tables where we could eat at chow time. It was a pleasant experience for me. The Aussie sailors were considerate, and the food was of good quality. The ship was pathetically slow, though. I thought a lot of the war would be over by the time we got there — a foolish thought, of course.

The last leg of the trip to Cape Gloucester was made on what I have always considered one of the most beautiful of ships, the APD *Noah*, an old destroyer. After the transports we were used to riding, it was sleek and fast. The crew was fast, too, and efficient with their guns and depth charges and such equipment. It all operated very smoothly.

One night as we sailed along in the darkness we began to hear the thunder of bombs and shells and see their flashes on the distant horizon. The navy radar had picked up Jap sub activity, and the *Noah* catapulted a series of depth charges. For better or worse, my time as a noncombatant would soon end.

In one little V-mail from about that time, I wrote a lot of trivia but ended:

> Dad and Mom, I've lived a lot for twenty-one years and been as happy as a human could be. You have been perfect. If something should happen, don't feel that life has slighted me. Two of my friends are singing harmony "if I could hear my Mother pray again." It is pretty.
>
> Jim

New Britain was a miserable son of a bitch from beginning to end. No matter how many high-powered machines were available to carry people about, when it came time to go into the war the line company fighters carried all they were going to need on their backs: whatever was necessary to protect themselves from the weather and to feed themselves, as well as the where-with-all to wage war. In other words, about all they could carry and still function halfway decently.

First it was over the side of the transports, down cargo nets under a load that made your legs, arms and lungs burn, so close to maximum effort that you feared you would fall. Then it was on to the beaches, where the really hard work began. There you would strain your ass off all day through the deep, sticky mud and jungle, then stand watch a third or half the night. Most of the days and nights it rained. What rest you got was generally in a hole full of water. Mosquitoes swarmed everywhere. If you swung your arm in a half circle, shoulder high, you would hit several of them. You always had prickly heat bumps. Leeches were everywhere, as were the black, scorpion-like bastards whose sting was so potent. It was a muddy slophole, the most miserable physical conditions I've ever been in. Lots of pretty tough guys completely crapped out.

So over the side of the *Noah* we went. From the nets we boarded the little landing crafts and hit the beach at Cape Gloucester. It was late December 1943. Some other parts of our unit had landed before us. Being a part of an invasion force — a landing force — created some new, rather heavy feelings. When I watched the magnificent green machine landing and deploying, I thought how glad I was not to be on the receiving end of that assault.

Where we landed on Cape Gloucester, there were bodies of some Jap soldiers at the edge of the water, where the ocean waves beat on the beach. The corpses lapped up and back in the waves. That seemed proper to me. That is why we were there — to kill Japs. A little farther up on the beach, we passed a stack of the bodies of some of the marines who had been killed in the original landing. It was very unnerving. Naturally, I was not so naive as to expect that I would not see such sights, but there is quite a difference between contemplating what might happen and the actual experience. The bodies were muddy and bloody, mutilated and pitifully ugly.

It was near the bodies that I saw Fitzgibbon and J. P. Cockrill, two friends of mine from Stateside duty who had been assigned to the First Marines. We had pitched some pretty wild liberties together in Dago. When my unit stopped near the stack of corpses I went over to talk to Fitz and J.P. They had been in the first battle there and you could see it in their faces. I asked how they were doing and Fitz answered, "Man, Jim, this is the shits."

He started to tell me about it, but we had only been there a few minutes when we got word to move out. That was the last I ever saw of them. Fitz was injured on New Britain and J.P. was later wounded on Peleliu.

Snipers and some heavier stuff began to harass our advance. Even though I wouldn't have wanted to be on the receiving end of the marine assault, I wasn't too thrilled to be on the receiving end of what the Japs had to offer, either. My education had begun, in a "tip-toe" fashion compared with what was to come, to be sure. But it let me know that when I joined the corps I hadn't had the slightest idea of what I was committing myself to.

As we continued to advance, we passed by a Jap artillery piece that had been taken. I was amazed at how small it was. It must have been between 50mm and 60mm bore size, but no longer than about four feet overall and probably about waist high. It was kind of a brown color. I was in hope that all their equipment was as junky as that piece looked. Later, I found out how wrong my impressions of the Japanese and their equipment were.

We got through the Jap defenses on the beach. They had many gun emplacements, pillboxes, built out of heavy coconut logs. For some reason they had chosen not to equip or man those positions, much to our joy and good fortune.

From this point the chronology of events is hazy to me, as are the exact locations, particularly through the first part of the New Britain battles. At that time I was always so involved in my own little job that I never seemed to know what the hell was going on. Things new to me happened too fast and too erratically for me to catalog them. Adding to this confusion was the nature of the deployment of the Jap defenses. Though there was the large concentration of enemy men and materiel at

Rabaul, their other forces on New Britain did not seem to follow any particular positioning. Not to me, at least. You were liable to run into them anywhere and anytime, and we did a lot of jumping around during the campaign.

As I remember it, the first or second day the Second Battalion, Fifth, along with some elements of the First Marines, secured the airport, on the coast, west of our landing area. From the airport we began a series of combat patrols through the swamps and rugged terrain inland.

It was tough for a newcomer to get his bearings, and the old guys didn't tell us all that they perhaps should have. I guess they couldn't tell us everything, and they probably thought we would learn from experience. Of course that was true, but once in a while experience was damn near too late.

Take, for instance, what happened one of the first nights we were on New Britain. I didn't have the slightest idea of where we were with regard to the land, or with regard to the other troops. All day I had walked near the tail end of a long column of men. In addition to my own personal gear (chow, water, rifle, ammo, grenades, and the like), I carried two boxes of machine-gun ammo belts, twenty pounds apiece, one in each hand.

The rifle was slung loose on my shoulder, flopping around. My hands and arms ached from the constant weight of the two heavy ammo boxes. After all the men in front of me had walked through the mud on the jungle trails, the tracks were always at least ankle-deep, and many times were nearly knee-deep. We had walked miles, during which we had to strain to pull our feet out of the sucking mud to make the next step.

When it began to get dark we stopped. We moved off the side of the trail and dug foxholes in the mud where we would spend the night. I didn't know where the Japs were or where other marines were. I was too intimidated and bashful about my ignorance to ask anyone exactly what the hell I was supposed to do. When it was my turn to stand guard, I sat up on the edge of my foxhole and peered into the darkness. It was very dark and I was very tired. It was extremely difficult to keep from dozing off. I did painful things to make myself remain alert. Sometimes I would bite my lip. Then I would stand up for a while. Sometimes I would hit my shins with my rifle butt. Knowing that my friends were entrusting me with their lives, I struggled to remain awake.

Then, suddenly, I was wide awake. I had heard something. Something had made a sound that was foreign to the natural sounds of the night. I was gripped with terrible doubt and dread.

What should I do? The old guys had warned me not to fire a weapon in the night if I could avoid it. Firing would make a flash that exposed your position. Throw a grenade first, if possible. That gave you a chance to neutralize your enemy and still keep your own exact position concealed. Besides, the night was so dark I could see nothing defined enough for a target.

I hoped that I was mistaken, that my imagination had been responsible for what I thought I had heard. Perhaps there was nothing there and all quiet would return to the night. I would be spared the burden of committing myself to a critical course of action that might be a mistake. I thought of awakening some of the others, but I knew how everyone hated the "nervous Gervase" who awakened us all at every strange sound.

Then the sounds came again. They were definite this time. Someone or something was moving near the trail. It was close to us. I heard a metalic "clink."

It was too late to awaken anyone else now. In my quandary I had waited too long to get any help. I was on my own. When I heard the first sounds, I had picked up a grenade from my gear. I thought, "Now, I have no choice. I wish to God I was somewhere else, but I'm not. If I don't get the bastard he will surely get some of us."

I pulled the pin on the grenade. At that moment a Georgia drawl broke the stillness of the night, "Baccigalupi, where the fawk is E Company?"

Oh, shit — I had dropped the pin! There I was, stuck with a live grenade and nowhere to throw it — nowhere I knew that would be free of marines. Any time I loosened my grip on the spoon of that grenade I would have three seconds to dispose of it, otherwise die and probably kill some of my buddies at the same time. So I held the damn thing till it got light enough to see where to dump it without the risk of hurting anyone.

Luckily, on that first night my watch was toward the end of the night, and I didn't have to hold the grenade too long. It was no big deal, really. For a little while, though, it was pretty dicey.

During those first days on New Britain I began to learn about the war, in little pieces and big pieces. Everything was so new and strange to me. I had no idea what to expect.

I was completely in awe of the big twin-engine Martin bombers that the army sent to bomb and strafe the hills in front of us, in preparation for an attack.

Most everywhere we went in the jungle we would eventually encounter snipers that were both efficient and difficult to locate. We learned not to let them stop us. We would leave some spotters to try to find them, and the rest of us would advance through the snipers.

In the corps the first letter of your last name will often dictate the men with whom you are associated. I went to lots of duty with a boy named Hill because *H* and *J* are close in the alphabet. He died from one of those snipers' bullets.

One day I saw a tree fall along the edge of a swollen stream. It hit a marine and killed him. How ironic! In the midst of all that war, a man dies from a tree falling on him.

There were some places you could see a long way, over beautiful grassy slopes and up into the hills. As I watched there one day, the mortars started exploding in the grass in front of us. One of my recurring bad dreams has always begun in that high grass, on some gently sloping hills on New Britain.

It was on the island that the boy died from the neglected jungle rot, as I wrote about earlier. I was around him quite a bit but for the life of me I can't remember his name. I do remember that there was too much war there to gloss over it in any historical account of the Pacific Theater.

After we had been there a few days, we made a combat patrol in the area of Borgen Bay. We slopped through the mire for twenty-six miles within Jap territory.

Utter led the patrol. He had come overseas as a corporal, an NCO transferred into an old outfit of privates and PFCs (privates first class) who had been with the corps overseas, in combat, a long time. The out-fit naturally resented his placement in a position of command, but be-fore we finished the patrol Utter had made believers of the old guys. He was the point — the lead man — for much of the patrol. Carrying a tommy gun (Thompson submachine gun), he killed several Japs during the patrol and governed himself throughout as a solid marine. I don't re-member any time or place thereafter that anyone, new or old, ques-tioned Utter's right to the rank and authority he had.

As we made our way through the slop, we came across a rather flat area that I think was a native graveyard. Every little way there was a wooden pole stuck in the ground and on the top of each pole was a shrunken human head. I don't know for certain if they were real but they looked like it, bushy hair and all.

As we passed by, a couple of the marines started shooting the heads off the poles. Everybody else yelled at the shooters. It wasn't that any-one regarded it as an impropriety. Shooting just got everybody on edge, worrying that there might be enemy troops around.

I remember place names I heard during those first days of patrols in-land from the north coast — Natano, Umboi, Aisega, Kara-ai, Garove, Agulupella — but I cannot be certain which of the places I was, or when. Studying such historical accounts as are available is of little help, be-cause as machine gunners we were with E Company much of the time, but on occasion we went with different outfits (with several different of-ficers) who needed our firepower. I don't believe some of the places we went had names but, to be certain, by any name those "roses" were just more jungle and coconut plantations. You could change the name of ev-ery damn one, and very few people on the face of the earth would know the difference.

We moved mostly east and finally wound up at a place called Iboki on the north coast. There we set up a perimeter defense and continued to patrol the hills in that area.

The days stretched on into weeks and months, with very few pitched battles like those we would have in later campaigns, but always some casualties. Guys getting wounded, guys getting killed, guys getting sick with new and old maladies. Everyone had black jungle rot on his feet and fungus in his crotch.

After several weeks of the campaign, during the first part of March 1944, it was decided to send some elements of the Fifth Marines up the coast to make a new landing. At the end of one long, arduous day we loaded up on a bunch of small craft to make the trip to a place called Talasea, on New Britain's Willaumez Peninsula.

My little unit went aboard a landing craft that I recall as an LCM (Landing Craft Medium), but I can't swear to its official designation. It was manned by an army crew. They were very competent, but the craft didn't seem big enough to be ocean-going and it was loaded so full of marines that we couldn't lie down. The craft had a bow end that could be lowered as a ramp to load and unload its cargo, of whatever kind. Outside the cargo well, high enough to be out of the water, there was a narrow catwalk, probably one and one-half to two feet in width.

We sailed all night, bobbing around in the blackness. I rode next to my squad leader, Corporal Morgan E. Gilmour. (He always said, "E, as in easy.")

Gilmour was from Marcellus, New York, and had been in the corps quite a while. He had been stationed at Guantanamo Bay, Cuba during the era when Hemingway lived and wrote there, and he told me many stories about marine liberty at Gitmo. Gil had curly, coal-black hair. He was a little bit of a dreamer and a good deal of a fatalist, and was real sharp about most everything.

Whenever the duty status would allow us time, he and I would ask the last night watch to wake us just before dawn. We'd get on a hilltop overlooking the ocean and watch the sun rise over the water. The contrasting colors of the island mornings were brilliant and beautiful. Our conversations there covered many and varied subjects but were mostly about life and the philosophies of society.

On one occassion I asked him, "What are you going to do after the war, Gil?"

"You're getting a little ahead of yourself, aren't you, Jim?" he answered. "I don't think it profits us much to try to see too far into the future. I think we're probably better off to talk about things that aren't dependent on time or fate."

We often spent much of the time in those brief respites without saying anything, engrossed in our individual thoughts.

Gil had been with the Division on the Canal and he sometimes told me things about that, but never in a condescending way. He was always considerate and tried to make our lives as good as he could under the circumstances. Besides being a capable and admirable squad leader, he was a real friend. He was one of the NCOs who strengthened my belief in the corps.

On the craft going to Talasea I was really tired. I told Gilmour I'd like to lie down on the catwalk but I was sure I'd go to sleep and roll off into the sharks. He said he'd watch me. He sat on a ledge on the side of the catwalk and held on to my belt to keep me from rolling into the sea while I slept. That's what we did and, though I didn't sleep long, it was enough to get rid of some of the kinks in my muscles.

In the morning when it got light, we were lolling around in the water a couple hundred yards off our proposed landing beach. There were several geysers of water from shellfire rising sporadically between us and the beach. I asked John Gibson what they were and he said, "They're big bastards — 90s at least, I'll bet."

We went on in and landed on the west coast of the peninsula, at Volupai. Some of our lead elements had stalled in front of us, and we didn't get off the beach as quickly as we should have. I was looking at one of our men lying on the beach a few yards away when one of the big Jap mortars lit on his belly. It blew pieces of him onto my cheeks and dungarees. I wiped the pieces off my face and scraped the chunks off my dungarees with my knife.

The explosion had separated the man's head from his body, and his head laid there on the ground by itself. I didn't see any other recognizable parts of his body. It was a ghastly sight.

We pushed inland and in the course of time came to a place called Bitokara Mission. There was a chapel there in an area where the jungle had been cleared. There was a grotto with a beautiful statue of Mary that was inspiring to me. Perhaps she was whispering to me of things to come.

Later we were moving in a staggered column along a narrow trail road that led up over a hill called Mount Schleuchter and to the villages at Waru, when we advanced into an ambush. When our lead elements neared the hilltop we drew artillery and mortar fire, and Japs deployed in the jungle along the road opened up on us with small arms.

It was late afternoon and our command decided we would withdraw to a tenable position, set up a perimeter defense for the night, and attack again in the morning daylight.

The machine gunners would cover the withdrawal. The procedure would be to use two gun crews to protect against counterattack while everyone else would withdraw down the hill to a nearly flat area, where we would set up night defense. One gun would set up on the road, near the top of the hill, while the second gun would set up about a hundred yards down hill. When everyone was clear, the first gun would break down, move down hill about a hundred yards below the second gun, and set up again. The second gun could then break down and move a hundred-fifty or two hundred yards farther down and reset. We would leapfrog in reverse.

I was in the first gun squad. I was an ammo carrier — about as near nothing as you could get as far as world opinion was concerned. But without my two boxes of machine-gun ammo, there would be a fucking bunch of marines with a lot better chance of dying.

When the second gun was set up, our gunner and assistant gunner broke our gun and pod apart. We ammo carriers then picked up our boxes and started the hundred-fifty yards or so downhill. There we'd be ready to load our gun when it was set up, ready to take the responsibility of keeping us all from being overrun.

When I started back down the hill with my two boxes of ammo, we were under fire. I passed a guy who had been wounded and was being carried out on a stretcher. He stopped me and asked if I would put his foot on the stretcher with him. It had been blown off and was lying on the ground near us, still in his boondocker (Marine Corps–issue field shoe). I couldn't see what it could hurt, so I picked up his foot and put it on the stretcher. Then I picked up my ammo boxes and started hustling to catch my gunner so I'd be ready with my ammo when they needed it.

I hadn't gone fifty yards when I ran into a shavetail.[1] He was a new one to me. I didn't recognize him as one of our officers. The poor guy was obviously scared shitless, like the rest of us. He was trying to act brave, maybe for himself, or maybe for some brass that was watching him. He took hold of my arm and said, "Hold up there, marine."

So I stopped and asked him what he wanted.

He said, "Now don't panic, marine. Let's not panic, here."

Jesus wept. I didn't know what he was trying to prove, but he was beginning to piss me off. I said, "Nobody's panicking, but if you don't need something I wish you'd get out of my way. If I'm not down to that gun with my ammo when they need it, somebody plumb out of patience is going to be coming up that hill after my ass."

I just stood there for a second. When he turned away, I took off. He sure as hell didn't inspire much confidence and I was glad to get away from him.

I went down the hill to where Himmelsbach had set up the gun and was waiting for my ammo. He, on the other hand, inspired a lot of confidence. He looked askance at me and I knew he was wondering where I'd been. I said, "Snatch, somebody better be watching that fuckin' second looie. He's liable to get a lot of people into trouble."

The lieutenant was an inexperienced young guy, like me, who had been sent to command a bunch of old salts who had already learned their lessons the hard way.

If you drew a green officer like him, you just had to hope he would have sense enough to keep low-key and listen to the old guys in his command, that he would listen until he knew as much as they did. If he didn't, you could only hope you'd live long enough for him to learn the difference between war school theory and the real thing, before he had wasted a bunch of his men.

We got set up along the flat area on the side of the hill and waited out the night, when there was sporadic fire but no heavy Jap attack. In the next couple of days we established a temporary base camp around Bitokara Mission and patrolled the area until we left there for another location. The Talasea campaign cost 140 men in a little over three days.

After weeks in New Britain's mud a realization fell on me. If the very best I could hope for would happen — that being I would live through my tour of the South Pacific war and eventually get home — my folks would be a lot older by the time I would see them next. The thought depressed me. I was not only taking a helluva risk that I would never get home at all, and submitting to a helluva lot of misery while I waited to find out, but I was also using up a helluva lot of precious time away from the folks, and college, and girls.

When I started to write these memories, I planned to say nothing about women, but in their absence they occupied so much of a young man's mind that it is difficult to make no mention of them at all.

My letters home occasionally contained comments about different girls. They were something civilized to write home about, though I knew better than to take anyone too seriously, or to think anyone would take me too seriously under those conditions. I had seen too many "Dear John" letters to expect anything faithful or lasting from young girls living in the environment that existed in the States at that time.

It wouldn't have been desirable to write about what I was doing even if I could have passed the censors. "You should have seen the Jap I shot today, folks. I hit him in the chest with a .45 slug. You could see his blood and flesh spatter on the bushes behind him." No, that wouldn't have fit at all. So I often wrote about the girls, knowing full well the futility of the writing. Of the many marines I knew who left a girl behind, only one had a girl that still acted, at least, as though she was waiting faithfully for him after a couple of years, when the guy finally went home.

As for me, there were "ten pretty girls on the village square," but I didn't kid myself about any of them. I was completely reconciled that after a few months' absence the heart may grow fonder, but the flesh starts looking for someone new to sleep with.

That whole process of being replaced was all that a realist fighting the Japs could expect. There was still plenty of booze flowing in the good old usa, and all the rest was still going on — dances and picture shows and parties, cafés and dinners out, back seats and parlor sofas and bedrooms. There were still plenty of available young men in the college reserves and in the category of essential workers, as well as large numbers of stateside, rear-echelon servicemen.

A heavy, fatalistic attitude was also prevalent among the majority of the young. Sometimes it was real, sometimes it was phony. It was a philosophy that said, "There's a war on and nothing is normal. Eat, drink, and be merry if you can, while you can, because this chance may be your last."

The noncombatant servicemen played that angle to the utmost degree and met with positive response in many quarters. Most girls were looking for an excuse, anyway, that would ease their consciences while they satisfied their physical appetites. And it was a pretty fair excuse, I guess. It sure was a natural consequence, under the circumstances.

A lot of people were getting fucked, many of *them* literally and many of *us* figuratively. But I'll let you in on a secret. When I think back about the girls that kept writing to me, I love every one of them. I appreciate them more than they will ever know. Even though I knew I was a real fool when I believed anything they were telling me. They have a place in my heart because they kept writing, and their letters came to me like a torch in the darkness. They let me know that somewhere there was still someone to whom I was more than just a serial number. More than a nobody in the hundreds of line company leathernecks[2] who would die in the mud with no one but their buddies beside them to even notice who was gone.

Remembering that reminds me of the Civil War soldiers who pinned name tags to their tunics when they started into the big battles. They did so because they hated the thought of someone looking at their bodies afterwards and not even knowing who it was who had died there.

The idea of dying at twenty-one years of age didn't much appeal to me, but the anonymity of dying among so damn many other guys that they piled your bodies in stacks was particularly revolting.

Another realization was that my conscience just wouldn't let me do some things no matter how extreme the circumstances. I was young and I did a few things in the corps that still embarrass me when I think back about them. For some time after the war was over, thoughts of some of those things were very disconcerting. As I have gotten older I have realized that I made some revolutionary changes in my life at that time to which I didn't adjust properly and timely. That contributed in part to my doing some inexcusably stupid things.

I went from a very sparsely populated area of Nebraska into the hordes of California. I went from a place where I was a schoolboy with a kind and loving home life into the bloody Marine Corps. I had no idea how to properly govern myself in an adult lifestyle, in a thickly populated area, under military authority.

I had not the slightest idea whose advice I should most honor, whose example I should try to follow in the corps. I had to learn some costly lessons the hard way. I had some NCOs subtly order me to steal, instructing me to replace my gear that had been lost or stolen by taking gear from other marines. It didn't take long for me to find out I couldn't reconcile my conscience to that. Swiping stuff as a schoolboy was bad enough to bother me forever. It was one thing to midnight-requisition stuff from the corps itself, but to steal gear from your fellow enlisted men was inexcusable.

We patrolled many miles of western New Britain's rugged terrain both before and after the battle at Talasea. Several times we set up bivouac areas because we were such long distances from territory over which we had complete control. We would set up outposts, generally two or three hundred yards out in the jungle from the bivouac area, to protect our bivouacs from surprise attack. We put two machine guns in each position. One gun would fire "free gun." That meant it was not locked down and could fire in any direction needed. The other gun would be staked to fire on a final protective line, or FPL. The gun staked for the FPL would fire across within a few feet in front of the next flank position. We would have a prearranged signal between the adjacent guns that let us know when to fire on the FPL. That signal would mean we were under heavy, close-in attack and the position down the line would fire its FPL mission a few feet in front of us. Quite a formidable setup.

Because of the danger of becoming disoriented and approaching from an unexpected direction when changing the watch on the guns, we would string wire from our bivouac through the bush to the gun positions. That lessened the chances of getting shot or attacked with hand grenades by our own men.

It rained almost incessantly. The guard watch in the muddy gun positions in the middle of the black-assed nights was miserable. Two men stood each watch. When it was time to change watches, one man would follow the wire from the outpost back to the bivouac area and awaken the next watch. The new pair would follow the wire out to the guns, hoping as they went that the lone man left on the guns hadn't been knifed or bayoneted while he was waiting. Hoping also that if he was still alive, he wouldn't spook when he heard his relief coming and shoot them, mistaking them for hostile troops.

The army had issued us jungle hammocks that were carried by headquarters personnel when we were actively engaged or moving. When time and conditions allowed, headquarters company would bring up our hammocks and we could hang them in the bivouac area. They were a welcome relief. We could string them between trees and thereby get off the wet ground. Attached to each hammock were zippered mosquito netting and a little waterproof canopy that draped over it. The hammocks were superb, very well designed. They would keep you dry and out of the mud, snakes, and mosquitoes, as long as you kept them in the proper attitude, horizontal like an airplane. Their only shortcoming was that they tore to pieces if they ever got out of that proper attitude. That meant you couldn't start a hammock swinging, sit down in it wrong, or do anything except lie quietly in it. Out of the proper attitude, you could tear it all to hell in a couple of seconds. There were no surveys[3] on hammocks. When you wrecked one you were SOL — shit out of luck.

In the wee hours of one night, a friend of mine named Zuka, who was from another squad, was asleep in his hammock. Suddenly Zuka yelled out in his sleep, in a voice clearly audible to the rest of us sleeping in the bivouac area, "Ease the pressure." Then he flipped over in his hammock, ripping it to pieces.

Zuka told us he had dreamed that Duke (one of his buddies) was flying an airplane and Zuka was riding straddle of the fuselage just in front of the tail. Duke started a steep dive and the pressure started to build up. That is when Zuka hollered and flipped his hammock. I suppose he had started to swing in it, either as a result of the dream or the cause of it. Anyway, he was out of a hammock. From then until Zuka went home, almost every time he came into sight someone would sing out, "Ease the pressure."

And then there was the hammock story that Frenchie told me as a joke on himself. Frenchie was one of my real close buddies whom I'll tell you more about, later.

In the course of events, Frenchie had somehow wrecked his hammock also and had no place to sleep. He told me he had come back from the outposts one dark, rainy night when he was wet and cold, and he decided to crap out for the rest of the night under the first hammock he came to. It was Himmelsbach's. Frenchie said he had crawled into a tight little curl, under Snatch's hammock, to try to keep warm and out of the rain. Snatch didn't know Frenchie was there. Frenchie said he was just getting settled when he heard Snatch unzip the mosquito net on his hammock. Frenchie said he was pretty sure Snatch was going to piss on him — and he did. I asked Frenchie how he reacted, and he said, "I just laid there. It was warm."

During one of the days back on New Guinea, I returned to our area after we had been on a conditioning patrol. I dumped my boxes of ammo and went back a couple of miles along our march route to help one of my buddies who didn't feel up to snuff. He had crapped out from fatigue. I picked up his boxes of ammo and carried them for him as we walked back to our company area. When I got back to the squad tent that served as our quarters, I passed a big Hoosier corporal who had gotten back earlier. He said, "For Christ's sake, boot, did you crap out on that little walk?" He turned to someone near him and said, "Things must be tough in the States. Look what they're sending us for men."

It was difficult to stomach his insults but I knew better than to say anything. He was big enough to beat me to a pulp, he was an "old guy" with time in the corps, and he was an NCO. There was no way I could win if I got smart-ass with him so I just walked on by without answering his taunt.

My chance came later. On one of our patrols on New Britain (real combat, no training exercise), it was very gratifying for me to pass him, crapped out to rest alongside the muddy trail through the jungle. I was carrying a full complement of gun ammo, besides all my own gear and weapon. Being an NCO, he carried only his gear.

As I walked past him, I looked straight at him and said, "This hiking tough on you big guys, is it, corporal?"

He looked daggers back at me, but he never answered.

It was my experience that many times (though not always) big guys had as much mouth as muscle. When the time came that I could pick replacements for my outfit, I usually picked from the little guys first. They were accustomed to taking more shit and often proved to be more durable. Frequently, I found that they stood up better in combat situations. In combat, how much bigger you were didn't mean how much more weight you could throw around, but only how much larger a target you were.

I had a close friend that I will refer to only as Stink. Because of some of the things I'll tell you about him, he might prefer that his true identity not be revealed.

We had started one of our patrols through new hill country on western New Britain when the lead part of our column was hit from the flanks by automatic weapons fire. Without orders or instructions, Stink flanked the Jap guns by himself. When the flurry was over, there were three dead Japs at each location, and old Stink came out of there carrying a Jap Nambu light machine gun by the handle.

I don't suppose Stink killed all the Japs by himself. (Like all good hero stories, his story leaves much to the telling.) In truth, a good portion of the dead Japs were probably killed in different ways, like fire from the riflemen at the head of our column, or grenades thrown by whomever. However, it was Stink who went in there alone and came out with the gun. If he had been in good graces with his command, his acts would surely have been recognized. They weren't, though. Stink got in the corps by choice — he had the choice of going to the pen for stealing a car or serving a hitch in the Marines. He wouldn't have gotten recommended for a medal if he had brought in Tojo himself.

Stink never had a chance in the corps, but he was great in his own right and his own way. He was brave and careless about his own destiny, far beyond the average. He wasn't limited in the scope of his own endeavor. At one place he commandeered a ten-wheel truck, bluffed his way into a chow dump, and loaded what he wanted that was handy. He brought the chow close enough to us that we could carry it to our area on our backs. Then he ran the truck into a ravine and left it. I asked him, why not take the truck back where he got it, and he said that would be a sure way to get caught.

When we got off New Britain, Stink took off over the hill. When they finally caught him, he was in Perth, on the west coast of Australia. To get that far on your own was a monumental accomplishment by any standards. When they caught him they brought him back to the corps's authority and, it is my understanding, sent him back to a stateside prison.

Stink knew a song I would love to hear him sing right now. It was quite a long ballad about O'Reilly's daughter and how the balladeer had made up his mind that he would shag her.

Stink had made some mistakes, to be sure, but he was deserving of a better end than landing in the brig.

I remember other bits and pieces of New Britain.

Sometimes, I suppose when the volcanoes were working, the earth would tremble and make you feel dizzy, like you were losing your balance. The first time that happened, I wondered if part of the island was going to break up and fall into the sea.

On one patrol I got a Jap sniper's rifle. It was smaller than most of their rifles and was like new. It had a beautiful orange-colored stock, an attached ramrod, and bayonet. I carried it many long, mountainous miles on patrol. When we returned to our area I took the little weapon down to the beach, where I traded it to a rear-echelon army cook for a bunch of chow and a handsome, gold Hamilton watch. On the way back I stopped and ate a whole can of quince jam I had gotten in the trade. I got very sick to my stomach.

I soon traded the watch to Stink for a pistol that a headquarters major had been wearing at the time. Stink lifted the pistol, and when I got it our gunnery sergeant decided he wanted it. I wouldn't give it up, and I made a bad shitlist that lasted until the gunny was gone. Stink got the watch wet, took it apart to dry it out, and couldn't get it back together. He threw the pieces in the bushes.

The beautiful little sniper's rifle was an ill-fated souvenir. I guess it would have been better for all concerned if I had left it on the sniper's body.

One night in a new area, a bunch of wild pigs foraged closer and closer to our gun. We weren't too sure whether the pigs would attack us if they got close enough to feel we were a threat to them, so we riddled them. Disease was so prevalent that we were afraid to eat them, but it seemed like a waste to me. It was from that area that Nesbitt, my buddy from Melbourne liberty, was evacuated with elephantiasis, which we called moo-moo.

One day we were in a rest area when an officer asked for a volunteer detail to handle the flag-raising ceremony. I was near enough to the officer that I could get in on it before the detail was full. That was one duty that always found plenty of willing hands. It was an inspiring occasion. It was the only time I ever had a chance to be involved in the flag-raising ceremony, and I was grateful for the opportunity. When it was over and I sat musing about the situation, I couldn't help but wonder how proper it was for me to feel the thrill that I felt raising my flag on another man's country. Morally, I imagine it was improper, but I couldn't help thinking that it beat the hell out of him raising his flag on my country.

There is not a lot else to tell about New Britain: It was, day after night after day, the same terrific exertion under the same miserable conditions.

Later in the war, when it rained so long on Okinawa that everything got soaked up, conditions were harsh, but nothing to compare with the insufferable days in New Britain's infested, muddy jungle mountains.

If the Japs had held the ordnance on western New Britain that they had on Okinawa, we would still be there.

I have learned since the war that MacArthur's staff gave serious consideration to sending the First Division on to make a new landing on the Gazelle Peninsula. The proposal would have required what was left of the Division to cross a two-thousand-foot mountain range, through miles of jungle, in the monsoon rains, to attack the base at Rabaul. The huge Jap complex of troops and materiel there would have obliterated the First Division. Luckily for us, the marine command and Admiral Nimitz got that idea shit-canned.

In four months or so, we had done about all that was expected of us so we were relieved by the army's Fortieth Infantry Division. We sailed for the tropical paradise of Pavuvu in the Russell Islands, to rest and to get refurbished for the next blitz.

Though I didn't know it then, I was one of New Britain's nonbattle casualties. I had begun to have chronic heartburn and indigestion. I didn't know what to do about it, so I just went on with my duties. It was at home, after the war, that I found out what was wrong. I was using the bathroom one morning in Nebraska when it felt like one of my intestines was coming out my rectum. Our old country doctor came to my house to check it out and found about five feet of worm hanging out my asshole. Lord only knows how much more there was or had been of that one, or how many different kinds of worms I had, to go with him. I had big ones and little ones. From the flies, or mosquitoes, or ticks, or leeches, or the local water, or something, I had picked up one hell of a dose of intestinal parasites. Of course I was no different from a lot of other guys who spent a long time in the filth and disease. All that shit went with the territory. Do you have a complaint, marine? See the Chaplain. He has a new supply of TS cards.[4] In the Russian marines, it's toughshitsky; in the Mexican marines, el tougho dungo.

5. Pavuvu: A Lull before the Storm

I HAVE NEVER DISCOVERED a satisfactory reason for sending us to the rat-infested swamp that was Pavuvu, instead of the well-established and well-supplied base at Mbenika, only a few miles away. I think it was probably because no one wanted a division of marines around in a peaceful area, using up a lot of the rear echelon's goodies.

It would have been nice if we could have landed in a decent place to rest for awhile and get some decent food, instead of dropping into the muddy mess on Pavuvu. There a division that had just spent four months on a jungle campaign would have to work for several weeks to prepare decent places to pitch squad tents, just to have a dry place to sleep at night.

We went about that duty like we went about most others, with our heads down and our necks bowed. After a time in the corps, a marine learns to think like a marine. At some point in his tour of duty he subconsciously develops a fatalistic resignation, and thereafter concerns himself very little with the profundities of life. Though he may have an awareness of such things as honor and fidelity and eternity, he applies himself primarily to the immediate and elemental pursuits of survival: Where is the water and food? How do we get it? What's the best way to stay warm and dry? Who's shooting at us, and from where?

After we had made Pavuvu into a livable, though dull and unpleasant place, I took a working party down to the beach to unload a ship that was docked there. One hold was full of green-painted wooden crates. On the boxes was stenciled in large white letters: "To the enlisted men of the 1st Marine Division[,] Compliments of the personnel of General Motors Corporation." The crates were full of bottled spirits — wines, liquors, and whiskeys. We hauled them all to the officers' bar, as we were ordered to do, and that is the last we ever saw of them or their contents. Legally, that is.

On Pavuvu, in the middle of a large area that had been cleared and mowed, stood a lone tent. It was the personal quarters of the colonel who was the CO (commanding officer) of the regiment. In it was one sack, a generator, and the only refrigerator I ever saw in the islands. In the fridge were several bottles of the aforementioned booze. Some of it was very fancy — bottles of chianti in woven baskets, sauterne, burgundy, and others I'd never heard of.

One of my favorite acquaintances was a boy named Conrady from Kewanee, Illinois. We weren't closely associated on a lot of occasions, but he was always fun to be around and was game for about anything. One marine used to say Conrady would steal anything he could carry, and what he couldn't carry he would sit down beside and claim.

In the wee hours of one brightly moonlit night, Conrady and I crept across the huge mowed area to the colonel's tent and opened the fridge door. When the light in the fridge came on, we quickly found the switch and depressed it. While the colonel slept, a few inches from where we worked, we lifted every bottle in the fridge and crawled, clinking and sloshing, across the seemingly endless private domain of the regimental CO.

Of course we knew we couldn't drink the stuff. We would certainly be caught if we did. But it was a pleasure just to possess it. After all, the juice had been sent to us. We buried it under a pile of coconut logs we had cut to clear our tent area. If the ravages of nature have not destroyed them, I imagine those bottles of fancy wine and liquor are still there, under the stack of coconut logs.

During the time of the United States' military encounter with Iraq, I saw media coverage of Bob Hope and his entourage going to the Persian Gulf area on the good ship USS *Peleliu*. I had seen Bob Hope in person on Pavuvu, a few hours before we were to embark for the Peleliu invasion. I read, long afterward, an interview with Bob. He spoke of Pavuvu and of looking out across the crowd of young marines headed for Peleliu. He specifically mentioned thinking afterward about the large number of them that were gone forever in the next few days.

For us masses of the marine line companies, it was truly inspiring to have people as famous as Bob Hope and his crew — Jerry Cologna, Patty Thomas and all — come and do a show for us. But closest to my heart was Frances Langford.

When she came out on stage to perform, everyone started shouting, "'Paper Doll'! 'Paper Doll'!" one of her big hits. She turned to look at Bob and the others. You could tell she was thinking, "Oh no — not Dolly again." She even said something to the effect of, "Aren't you tired of that one?"

But the boys kept it up — "'Paper Doll'! 'Paper Doll'!" So she held up her hands to quiet them and started. She must have sung it hundreds of times before, and it surely must have been getting old for her, but you would never have guessed it from her performance. She belted it out like it was the first time she had sung it, for some New York audience. When she finished, the marines roared their approval for several minutes.

But what makes me remember her most happened when the show was over. They had flown over to Pavuvu from Mbenika in light planes, I think one passenger to each plane. When it was time for them to leave, they went back to the road that was used for a landing strip and got into their little aircraft. Crowds of marines followed them to the waiting planes. As much as I wished to see them closer, I had had all the push-and-shove crowds I needed, so I went alone down to the other end of the road, thinking I could at least watch them fly past. I'm sure none of the marines noticed which way the wind was blowing — for certain I didn't. As it happened, the plane carrying Frances Langford taxied down the road, turned into the wind for takeoff, and stopped not more than fifty yards from where I stood alone. She looked out the window and waved at me — not at five thousand bellowing marines falling over one another — but at one lonely asshole.

She may not even have realized that she was waving at just me standing there alone, but *I* did. I'm sure she didn't remember it the next day, but even if I were to live ten thousand years I would never forget it.

Not long afterward, we were on the transports, headed for the next blitz.

6. Hell Has a Name: Peleliu

THE LAST LETTER I wrote before we hit Peleliu is dated September 9, 1944. Writing it was quite difficult. We men were all familiar with what had happened at Tarawa, and we knew that what we were heading for would be a bloodbath. As much as I wished to spare the folks undue concern, I did not want them to receive a blunt notice of my death, followed by a letter filled with inconsequential banter, as though I had been ignorant of what we were going to be doing.

> Dearest Mom and Dad,
>
> I have received your mail in good order and hope my few letters have reached you alright.
>
> I told [a girl] goodbye. It is just as well because if anything should happen to me it would be hard for her to get over it. If I don't get through this time write her and say that I didn't intend to be mean but that it is best that we part and say goodbye.
>
> We are aboard ship going to a place you'll probably hear about before (if ever) you get this letter. Quite a lot of us have been in it before so we know what is coming. If you are going to draw a deuce from fate's deck then "C'est la guerre." One cannot live forever.
>
> Now do not worry because when you get this it will all be over and everything happens for the best.[1]
>
> As I write, I realize well that this may be my last letter. I, too, am without illusions but my love for you keeps me at peace. I am

not afraid and I am happy for I know that some greater day, whether here or on the other side, we shall meet again.

Until that day I am the one who loves you two more than all else.

Jim

In the corps there was a running, idiotic argument over purely imagined differences in worthiness between the regulars, the reserves, and the men who entered the service through the draft. I purposely did not use the word "draftees" because it was my understanding that even among the men drafted to serve their country, marines had voluntarily chosen the corps as the place they would serve, rather than some other branch of service. However true that was, the regulars were always accused of joining the corps because they couldn't make a living on the outside, the reserves were criticized for joining the corps so as to escape the unpredictable draft, and the drafted men were derided as a bunch who didn't help until they had to. As for me, when I enlisted in the corps I had first to get a release from my county board, meaning that I probably would have been drafted before long, anyway. Certainly most all able-bodied young men in that age group at that time were registered, and if they didn't enlist, they would no doubt soon be drafted.

During my tour of duty in the Marine Corps, I was always reluctant to make any derisive generalizations. I couldn't see any difference between the bravery and competency of men from the old corps and the men who came in at the last. Both groups — the new and the old — served with honor and sacrifice, and I knew well men from both who would have been a credit to any fighting unit ever put together. I always felt that only someone in careless thoughtlessness, or with callous indifference to the truth, would ever place either group above the other.

When we hit the beach on Peleliu, the outfit was pretty equally divided in number of old and new guys. I had been in the Pacific Theater about sixteen months. Some old guys had been there over two and a half years, whereas some of the new ones had only been with us a few days.

I got my first look at Peleliu on the morning of the day we landed, September 15, 1944. It was different from any environment we had seen before. Our previous campaigns had been on large islands that from the ships looked like they were all jungle and, for the most part, had been.

Peleliu was in the Palau Island group, which was part of the Western Carolines. It was a small, coral atoll about five miles long and in many places only about a thousand yards wide. When the sun came up that fateful morning, the island looked something like a burned matchhead or a clinker left in an old coal furnace. It proved to have about the same consistency as a clinker, also. It was extremely hard to dig into in most places, and the spiny coral would cut into you whenever you knelt or laid against it. One of the odd little things I remember about the island is the mat of twigs that lay thick on the ground almost everywhere that shell fire hadn't blown them away. About the size of a person's little finger, they were a residue of plant growth different from any I had ever seen.

As we watched the heavy, boiling smoke clouds rise over the island from the preinvasion naval bombardment, we didn't see how any human being on the place could still be alive. Unfortunately, the Japs were dug in so well, their positions fortified by the coral, that even that terrific shelling hadn't been able to put much of a dent in them.

Early that morning I had gone through the usual gut-wrenching trip over the side of the transport and down the cargo net into the little landing craft. Besides the clothing and helmet that I wore I carried the following gear: backpack with entrenching tool (mine was a shovel), one poncho, three light and three heavy rations, two packs of cigarettes in a waxed paper sack, a small leather case filled with weapons-cleaning gear, one extra pair of socks, one gas mask, one cartridge belt, one personal sidearm with two extra ammunition clips, one sterile canned compress, two canteens of water, one GI knife, two fragmentation grenades, and one Browning light machine gun, model 1919A4 (weight: thirty-six pounds). I carried two additional objects the corps probably would have confiscated as contraband if they had known about them: one pair of binoculars that I had picked up on New Britain and one s&w .38 Special, for which I had traded a navy pilot a good Jap battle flag.

Partway in to shore we transferred into amphibious tractors (amphibs) and bounced and wallowed precariously over the coral reefs that threatened to strand us in the water tearing holes in the amphibs or by high-centering them. My unit landed about an hour after the first wave, on the west side of the island directly west of the airfield. Taking the airfield was our first objective.

When we reached the shore and disembarked, I saw one hell of a sight up and down the beach. The sand was already littered with dead and mutilated bodies of U.S. marines — bodies of old salts and new selective service recruits lying side by side. You couldn't tell one from the other. All the armored amphibs that I could see had been knocked out and were burning. We went into the attack immediately.

It is my understanding that when we got ashore, the plan called for the element on our left to turn inland to the left, the element on our right to turn inland to the right, and for us to charge inland, filling the gap between. But plans and tactics seldom drift down, or mean much, to the rifle company enlisted men. These men just win the wars, they don't have to figure them out. As far as that goes, based on most things I've read, I think that history's greatest tacticians have proven to be ones with the most brave men, the biggest reserves of supplies, and perhaps their most important asset, the great good fortune of doing whatever chanced to be right at the time.

As I stood there on that beach, it didn't seem to me that our attack had worked out quite as planned. Nowhere could I see that anyone had gotten across the beach and through the little strip of brush that was between the beach and the airfield. Mortars and artillery rounds landed up and down the length of the beach. Automatic small arms fire came at us from the high ground on our flank. We advanced through the fire across the beach as rapidly as possible. When we reached the cover of the brush strip we stopped. Everywhere people were trying to figure out where everybody was (both our elements and theirs) and what the hell was going on.

When we stopped, I was standing beside a small path through the bushes. As I looked down at the path I saw a partially exposed mine a foot or so in front of me. As I stood there waiting to begin our advance again, a young company runner came down the path. As he neared me I could see he was intent on doing his job — probably trying to get information from other units to orient his people in charge — and wasn't aware of the mine. Thoughts ran quickly through my mind. If I hollered he might not notice me among all the other noise, and even if he did hear me he would just as likely jump on the damn thing as away from it. So I hit him across the chest with my machine gun in a way that knocked him clear of the mine. He scrambled up with a quizzical look on his face and said, "Hey, what's the matter with you?"

I said to him, "Sorry mate, but look," and I pointed at the mine.

His eyes opened wide. He grinned sheepishly at me and mumbled his thanks. He gave the mine a wide berth until he was past it and then hustled on down the path out of sight.

Pretty soon we moved out on the airfield. I was glad to get away from there. I had kept thinking that maybe the mine was on a timer or a remote control. It seemed so foolish to just stand right there by it, wondering if and when it was going to go off.

Crossing the airfield lengthwise didn't really seem like the brightest thing I'd ever done, either. It meant charging across approximately two thousand yards of flat ground, completely exposed to an enemy who had all kinds of firepower and control of the high ground, where he could watch every move we made.

I remember the desolation of both the place and my feelings when I looked out across the airfield and knew we had to try to get all the way across it. Through the shimmering heat waves I watched the dust and smoke rise from the mortar and artillery bursts detonating on the strip. As lethal as those bursts looked, and as lethal as I knew they were, I also knew that what would probably get the most of us would be the automatic weapons I could hear rattling sporadically but incessantly as we tried our advance.

Our gas masks were cumbersome, awkward to carry, and too heavy to drag along if they weren't needed. We always figured that if the enemy didn't gas us when we landed, the chances were good that he never would. So we didn't ordinarily keep the gas masks very long. In the interest of maneuverability and a better chance to stay alive under fire, we would dump them.

We hadn't been on the beach at Peleliu very long before we realized that we stood a lot better chance of getting killed from weapons fire than from being gassed, so we had dropped off the masks along the way. When we had traversed the width of the airfield, made a ninety-degree turn, and were about halfway down its length, we became aware of a large, green cloud of smoke or vapor. It was lying along the side of the hills in the direction we were headed and it looked suspiciously like gas. The word passed down to us to prepare for a gas attack. If we went back after our masks, though, we would surely lose all the ground we had taken. There would have been panic. Quickly devising a scheme, we set up strong points to hold what ground we had taken, and a few men went back to pick up masks for us all. As it turned out, there was no gas attack. The green cloud soon dissipated and before long we threw the masks away again.

I think what had happened was that some of our shelling had hit some of their ammunition and it exploded, loosing the green smoke. The explosive in some of the Jap shells left green smoke, where as ours, and others of theirs, made black smoke. I was to see that green smoke many times thereafter but never again in that magnitude, all in one concentration. I was told, correctly or incorrectly, that the explosive was picric acid. Whatever it was, it had a distinctive smell. Once you had been around the devastation, your belly would get tight whenever you smelled it.

By the grace of God, some of us got all the way across the airfield. It was late afternoon and it had taken us most of the day to advance to that point, but we had a salient into the enemy-held territory. At the very point of that salient we set up our gun to keep the Japs from taking back any of the ground that had been so hard for us to get. The E Company squad leaders who had led our attack across the airfield positioned fire teams with BARs (Browning Automatic Rifles) on our oblique flank to support the gun.

Now, as I write, many thoughts come to mind almost at once, faster than I can write. I must caution myself to slow down so that I write complete thoughts, coherently. My inclination is to write very rapidly in order to put something to paper while it is still in my mind.

As I wrote earlier, when I first went overseas the machine-gun squads had been in the weapons companies. There were some tough times for sure, but we had been, in truth, support troops. We went with the rifle company platoons only when they needed us. Immediately after the New Britain campaign our organization changed. The atoll landings and the progression of the island war demanded immediately available maximum firepower. As I have said, the machine gunners were transferred permanently to the rifle companies, and the battalion weapons companies, D, H, and M, were disbanded.

During campaigns thereafter the machine-gun sections constantly accompanied the rifle platoons. The rifle squads and the machine-gun squads mutually supported one another. The heavy machine guns (water-cooled) were boxed and carried by some later-arriving echelons in case we ever needed them. To my knowledge they were never used after that campaign. We carried only the light guns (air-cooled).

When we heard of the plans for this new organization and deployment, we were fully aware of what was to come. We would charge along with, or very close to, the rifle squads so that we could deploy and bring our automatic firepower to bear on the enemy in a matter of seconds. To defend what ground had been taken, we would man the high ground and the points of deepest penetration into enemy territory. We had known there would be some grim times.

This was the case when we found ourselves on the far side of the airfield. We set up our gun at the point of deepest penetration.

Three of us were very close together at the gun position — Charlie Smith, Jimmy Miller, and I. Charlie Smith, from Lawrenceburg, Tennessee, was our squad leader. He was a big, good-looking boy. Miller and I were the gun crew. He was gunner and I was assistant gunner. He was from Lexington, Kentucky, just a little way from where my folks were then living. He was very young and for that reason we called him "Chick," as in young chicken. They were both quiet guys, easy to get along with but totally accountable in any situation. Smith dug in on our left side and Miller and I were on the gun.

We set up the gun on the edge of a small clearing in the brush, behind a little pile of sand we found there, as near the pile as we could put it for maximum protection and still be able to maintain an effective field of fire.

It was a very small sand pile, really. It was shaped a bit like a cone with a rounded or worn down point at the top. It was about two feet tall and probably four or five feet across at the base. As I said, quite small for a sand pile, but as far as my life was concerned it was as big as the Rock of Gibraltar. Without the presence of that pile of sand I am satisfied I would have been killed on many different occasions that first night on the island. All through the night, bullets, grenades, and mortar shrapnel pounded into the sand pile as the Japs tried to neutralize our little slaughter machine.

It was a long, miserable, sleepless night. We started to try to stand 50 percent guard, but there was too much activity. No one could sleep. Even though there had been no practical opportunity to eat, hunger was not really of too much concern, as yet. In the sweltering heat and hard work of battle, we had each consumed all or most of our water, and that was a serious concern. We had practiced water discipline at great length in the States and we had been short of water in battles before, so we knew what to expect. But the body demands water. No amount of practice can change that. No matter how strong your will or how controlled your mind, you either drink what water you have or die in not too long a time. I always tried to set a goal when water was short. I would try to wait until four o'clock in the afternoon before I took the first drink because when you have once tasted the water, it is very, very difficult to stop drinking.

I still had a little water left that first night but I soon began to wonder about the practicality of saving it. It would seem ironic to die thirsty, from a bullet, with half a canteen of water at your side, but Grandpa Johnston used to say, "You must prepare for tomorrow even if you die today." So I drank the precious stuff, one sip at a time, and then screwed the top back on my canteen quickly so I wouldn't gulp down the rest of it.

The Japs started to pressure us by individual and small group probes and our gun position on the point almost always took the first contact. We tried to neutralize them at first by calling for artillery and mortar support fire. Our marines in those units were extremely talented, and for a while we could stop the Jap movements with that support and with

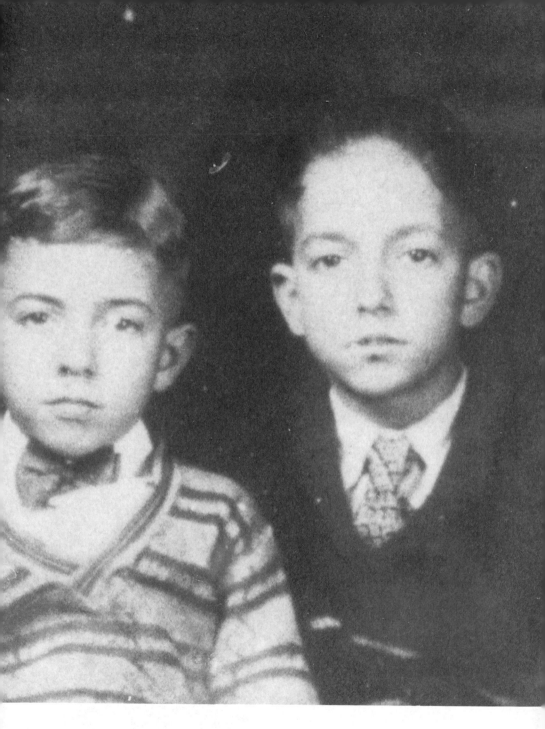

Jim Johnston, age 6 (left) and his brother, Josh

Jim Johnston, age 16, on motorcycle in front of boyhood home in Wauneta, Nebraska

Jim Johnston, age 20, in San Diego, California, prior to going overseas

Leon Utter, Fifth Marines
(Photo courtesy Leon N. Utter)

Joe Lunsford, Fifth Marines
(Photo courtesy Joseph N.
Lunsford)

Bob Miles, Fifth Marines,
wounded three times in battle.
(Photo courtesy Robert W.
Miles)

Jack Howell, Fifth Marines,
killed in action on Okinawa

grenades. Soon, however, we had to use our individual weapons, and before long they sent attackers at us in such numbers that only the machine gun could stop them. That made our position clearly defined, and the Japanese sent everything they had at us. So we spent the night hungry, thirsty, and very tired. We were really weary, but we knew that to relax a few seconds would probably cost us our own lives along with the lives of several of the riflemen who looked to us to carry our share of the load. It was our day in the barrel. We killed Japs with everything we had. We killed them all around us all night long. We killed them in small groups trying to sneak through us and in masses trying to overrun us.

We expended all the ammunition we carried. Utter, our platoon sergeant, didn't ordinarily move with the assault sections but he knew we were running out of ammo. In the middle of the night he came up carrying all the belts he could. As he neared us he called out, "Here comes Santa Claus." At the time he looked much better than Saint Nick. Gibson, a platoon sergeant from another company also knew our plight, and in the night he also came to our position carrying several belts of ammo wrapped around his shoulders. He dropped his ammo belts near the gun. He tapped me on the shoulder and said, "Give 'em hell, boys," then faded away into the darkness behind us.

No one who was not there can possibly imagine the feeling those men created, the lift in spirit they gave us. It was a thrill and a great inspiration to know that they were behind us with all the physical aid they could muster and all the spirit they could summon up.

To keep the ammunition belt running in the gun, I had to lie at a ninety-degree angle to its direction of fire. To watch our targets and to be able to see what I shot with my pistol, I had to keep my head turned sideways. We ran twenty-one boxes of ammo through that magnificent little machine gun that night and killed Japs by the stack — some in front of us and some behind. I had gotten so stiff in the neck and back from looking over my shoulder for so long that I rolled over on my back against the sand pile to get a little rest. The bullets from an automatic weapon hit the pile and blew sand in my face. I looked up into the small bushes behind me and saw a little bird, about like a sparrow, flitting back and forth on the branches as the bullets snapped twigs around him. For a second I thought, "Sweet Jesus, little bird, if I had your wings I would fly the fuck out of here."

The Japs were starting another Banzai[2] attack against our gun position. I turned around and began again to feed belts of 30–06 into the little gun.

Miller moved the gun from behind the protection of the sand pile to a nearby foxhole vacated by a casualty. He hoped to have a better field of fire against the defilade in front of us. I crawled across the few yards to where the gun was so that I could shake the sand out of the ammo belts as they fed. I lay out on top of the ground completely exposed, and though I was snake-flat on my belly, it seemed like I stuck up like the "shithouse in the fog."

Miller tried to pick up the gun and hold it so as to get a better angle at the low ground in front, and I tried to carry the ammo belt so that it would feed properly but we were not very effective that way. The gun bucked around too much and was soon too hot to hold. We sat the gun back on the ground and continued to fire.

That place, during the first night on Peleliu, is the location of one of my recurring dreams — the dream about the waves of Japs that charged at us screaming "Banzai!" in their little high-pitched voices.

I have seen Major Gordon Gayle, who was co of the Second Battalion, Fifth Marines, quoted as saying that there were no overwhelming Banzai attacks on Peleliu that night.

I saw Major Gayle there early in the evening. When we had gotten all the way across the airfield that first day, he came up to see where we had our line and gun position. He had a bullet crease through the top of his helmet. It looked like the sniper had missed getting him by three or four inches.

I had held respect for Gayle before that time, but I developed more after he put in an appearance there.

However, though there might not have been any overwhelming attacks wherever the major was that night, for sure he hadn't stayed with us. It was after Gayle had gone back to his command post that the Japs started their Banzai counterattacks. There were three against our position, not overwhelming but nearly so. Perhaps what he meant by saying no "overwhelming" attacks was that none of them had been successful.

A Marine Corps dispatch concerning the part of the battle in which we participated that night was sent to a newspaper in my home state, the *Louisville Courier-Journal*. The newspaper published an article headlined "2 Kentuckians and Tennessean Kill 120 Japs, Marine Fire Turns back 3 Counterattacks."

The text of the article is reproduced here:

> One hundred twenty Japanese fell before the incessant firing of two Kentucky marines and one Tennessean during a recent dusk-to-dawn encounter on a formerly Jap-held island in the South Pacific, a Marine Corps dispatch disclosed yesterday.
>
> The leathernecks are Pfc. James W. Johnston, Columbia, Pfc. James W. Miller, Lexington, and Cpl. Charles K. Smith, Lawrenceburg, Tenn.
>
> At sundown of the day of the first marine assault on the island the marines had pushed from their beachhead into thick jungle growth, fighting fiercely for every yard, the dispatch said.
>
> Expecting Jap counterattacks after dark, the three marines dug in on the left flank of their line. The first attack came shortly after midnight. It was repulsed. A second and stronger attack followed and was repulsed.
>
> Just before dawn, the Japs staged a final frenzied attack which carried almost to within arm's length of the three gunners before their relentless and withering fire could halt it. In the morning, the three marines counted 120 Jap dead in front of their position.

The dispatch didn't say anything about it, but among that bunch of Japs there were three well-equipped machine-gun crews.

Neither did the dispatch mention that during the first twenty-four hours that the assault sections of machine guns in E Company spent on the island, one-fourth of our men were killed and many more wounded.

Someone told me that our company had forty-five casualties in less than an hour. Most all of them were from Jap machine-gun and rifle fire. Those gunners who died were close friends of mine, and I would never lie or exaggerate about them. Should anyone doubt anything I've said or wonder anything about our men's names, numbers, or dates of death, all the information can easily be substantiated in several places in the Marine Corps records.

During the time we were in that position, I shot three Jap soldiers with my .45 pistol. The first of the three was the first man I had ever killed. That is to say, the first one that I knew for certain that I and I alone had shot. Earlier in the war, the men we had been killing were a fair distance away or were the targets of much shooting. It had been impossible to tell who shot whom, but not in this case. The Jap was so close I could easily have spit on him. It is one of my most vivid recollections of the war and of my life, for that matter.

In the bush at night the Japs would send infiltrators against our lines and positions, both to do what damage they could and to establish what our location was. When this movement began, we could call for flares. Flares were shells that could be fired by either artillery or mortars. They would burst high above us, releasing parachutes that would open, having flares suspended from them. The lighted flares would drift down slowly and light up the area for a little while. The parachutes popped in the air when they opened and anyone would soon learn that seconds after the pop, the area was going to be lighted. So, to minimize the chance of being seen, you learned to freeze, motionless, when you heard the pop. Naturally, the Japanese soon learned the same thing. Sometimes if you happened to get caught in an exposed position, you might as well run like hell and take your chances.

Behind the little sand pile, when one of the flares above us burst, there was the Jap, almost beside me — maybe four feet away, at most. He had approached at a ninety-degree angle to my line of sight in watching for them to appear. He could easily have reached me with his sword. If he had seen me first, I would have had little chance. As it was, I had been close to the ground in a crouched position and he was standing. The flare didn't go off close to us, and I saw him first, silhouetted against the dim light. There had been activity already, and I was carrying my .45 ready as I watched. When the flare lighted, the Jap stood motionless — a perfect target. In a few seconds he was dead. I can still plainly see the spectral look of him in the pale, blue light of the distant flare as I pulled the trigger on the faithful little 1911 Colt.

The other two Japs I shot later, as morning broke, and the recollection of them is nearly as vivid.

There were a few times, not many but a few, when even my own life was subordinate to my purpose. That morning was one of them. Most of the times that I subrogated my own safety to something else, it was to get some of my men who were wounded to a place where the proper people could take care of them, but not this time. Risking your ass to save a wounded buddy was standard procedure in the corps. It was routine. That morning I wasn't thinking of saving one of my friends. I was killing and helping kill as many people as I could just as fast as I could. That is all I was thinking. In retrospect I feel a twinge of guilt or shame, at least of wonder, at the exhilaration I felt when at last I could blow away some of the people that had caused us so much pain and sorrow.

We had been fortunate in setting up our gun in a position that had a very good field of fire. There was, however, one small rise in the ground about thirty or forty yards in front of the sand pile where we had set up the gun. In one of the charges against us, this one shortly after sunrise, two of the Japs stopped behind that little rise. I was watching closely and saw exactly where they stopped. You calculate rapidly in a place like that or you are too late. I knew that if I took the time to pick up a grenade from the edge of the sand pile and throw it, the Japs would have time to throw grenades at us. So, recklessly, I stood up, hoping I could see them. From my standing position they were plainly visible where they lay on the ground. I held my .45 in both hands, aimed steadily, and shot them both. When the .45 slugs hit them, they bounced off the ground as though some giant had grabbed the back of their tunics and given them a flip. Charlie Smith brought me to my senses when he hollered, "Sit down, Johnston, you're drawing fire!" Until then I had paid little or no attention to the bullets that were popping the air close around us.

When I was down low to the ground again, I silently said my thanks that my unconsidered conduct had not cost me my life. I did get the Japs and kept them from getting us, but it would probably have been much more sensible and certainly much safer to have used the grenades. Having exposed myself as I did to the rifle and automatic small arms fire that was coming at us from the woods on the other side of a little clearing, I was lucky I didn't get shot.

We had accomplished our first day's objective and we held our position in spite of the intensity of the Jap counterattacks and the severity of our casualties. Later on Peleliu we found some printed matter written in Japanese that an interpreter read to us. In part, it said that the Americans' most effective weapon was their light machine gun and that in order to defeat the marines, the light machine guns must first be destroyed. From the way they came at us that night, I guess they must have believed it.

The second day on Peleliu, the word came down to get ready to move out. It sounded like a death sentence and for many of us it was. On command we were to fire what ammo we could into the bush across the clearing and then be ready to continue the assault. We had fired so many rounds during the night that the barrel in our gun was practically a smooth bore. Every fifth round in the belts was a tracer. When we started to fire that morning, the rounds came out in a wildly scattered pattern.

When ordered to cease firing and advance, I tried to pick up the gun. It was still very hot and burned the palms of my hands. I finally took hold of the grip with one hand and put my foot under the hottest part to raise the gun off the pod. In that way I could sling it one-handed on my shoulder across my pack and pack strap. Then we charged across the clearing and into the jungle on the other side. It was in this small area that many of the men in our sections died. Harold Goodey and Jack Sutton were killed in our night position. Clarence Maine, Orville Cook, and my buddies Himmelsbach and Moise were killed at close quarters by Japs who ambushed them after they had crossed the clearing. When we had established a position, I went over to see if I could do anything for Himmelsbach. He was still gasping but it was only reflexes. He had about thirty holes in him, of which roughly half were bayonet wounds.

Up until then my recollection of chronology is very good, but I had then been without rest for a long time. I had slept very little the night before we landed and none on the first night we were there. I was extremely tired from the intensity of both the heat and our activity. Many things happened in the few days that it next took us to fight our way across the island. They are vivid in my mind, but in recounting them I am very reluctant to say the exact sequence of the events.

Frenchie was caught in the same ambush that killed Himmelsbach and the boys. The ground we were moving through was heavily overgrown, and the Japs could get on you almost before you knew it.

As I wrote earlier, Frenchie — Jack Gene French — was one of my close buddies. He was about as ordinary looking a man as you'll ever find. He was about average in height and weight — maybe even a little shorter than average. You would never notice him in a crowd, even a small crowd. He wasn't homely, but he wasn't handsome either. His hairline had receded a little more than you'd expect for someone as young as he was. He was very quiet, didn't talk much. When you first met him, you might think he was inclined to be introversive. I had known him quite a while before he began to open up. You had to know him a long time, through places where life and death mixed intimately, before you realized what an extraordinary person he was on the inside.

You could count on Frenchie always to do the best he could in any situation. He had tenacity, the kind of courage it takes to be always where you're needed, no matter how long, no matter how futile or miserable are the prospects.

When the Japs hit, Frenchie was wounded. He still managed to get out for help, and he led the attack back in there three times to carry out his wounded and dead buddies. He had quite a lot of grenade shrapnel in his legs and back, and he went to the evacuation ship. If you didn't know the whole story, you'd think lucky Frenchie, because he got off Peleliu in a couple of days. Though he was wounded and almost all the rest of his squad had died, he was out of the war for a while. He was lucky to be alive. He was really lucky to get out of that chaotic hellhole in a matter of hours.

He'd been over there quite a long time, and when he left I hoped that he had a ticket home. That was not to be, though, damn it all to hell. After Peleliu was over, Frenchie came back. He led one of my sister sections of guns on Okinawa, and that's where he was killed. His civilian job before the war had been scooping coal to a blast furnace. In Gary, Indiana, if I remember right. (I hope and pray he's done with that activity.)

God, how I loved Frenchie. His mother wrote to me from Terre Haute, Indiana. I tried to find her after the war but I couldn't.

The terrain where Frenchie was wounded was a shallow ravine heavily overgrown with trees and vegetation of about every kind. It ran along the end of the airfield. As the fighting there progressed, after French and the boys had gotten out everyone they could, we advanced along the rim of the ravine. When we moved into strong resistance, someone called up a 37mm cannon and crew. We were firing our machine gun to keep the Japs occupied while the cannon crew got into position.

They set up right beside us and it was very interesting to watch their operation. They fired canister into the little ravine, which was very effective. (A canister load was like a large shotgun shell. It contained many small projectiles, whereas the usual artillery round contained but one.) They cleared a lot of the jungle and they drove a lot of Japs out of hiding. At that time the machine gun again became efficient.

We operated in that way for an hour or so. When it seemed we had the resistance neutralized, other troops assumed the point and began to advance. There were still many Japs in the rough coral lining the walls of the ravine, where we hadn't been able to get at them, and they proceeded to give the new point unit a sound pounding. The marines got through, but as they went they had a lot of casualties.

From our position on the edge of the ravine, we could see the stretcher bearers starting out of the depression. Several of them passed us. On one of the stretchers was a good friend of mine, Foster. He was a tall, slim, slow-drawling southerner, from Louisiana I believe. His father was a minister, and it was my understanding that Fos had begun some kind of apprenticeship as a preacher before entering the marines. You would never have guessed that from his demeanor or the language he used. His expressions were highly colorful, full of curses that were excessively lewd and abundant, even by Marine standards. It was obvious that when Fos joined the corps, he aimed to leave all vestiges of the ministry behind. Naturally, he couldn't do that. He had come from a good, kind environment and its influence was too deeply impressed upon him for him to be able to abandon it entirely. He was a good boy and a conscientious marine. Only his talk mirrored his revolt against convention, and it was fun to listen to his prodigious swearing.

When the stretcher bearers carrying Foster got out of the ravine they stopped close to me. I went over to look at him. His upper arms and chest were pretty bloody, but he was conscious. When he noticed me standing over his stretcher, he said, "Look, Johnsey." He opened his hand and in it was the bullet-riddled remains of the little metal-framed Bible he had carried in the chest pocket of his dungaree jacket.

There was not much tact employed among the troops in the Fleet Marine Force, and I said bluntly, "I see it. How you doing, Fos? Are you going to make it?"

The bearers picked him up then, to start off, but he looked back and said, "I don't know Johnsey, but if I do I'm going back to preachin'."

That was the last I ever saw or heard of him. I have often wondered whether he made it, and if he did, whether he went back to "preachin'."

That evening I was trying to dig a hole in the coral as a night position. I had traded my shovel for a pick because we couldn't dig in the hard rock with anything but a pick. My hands were blistered and sore from picking up the hot gun, and the jar of the pick as I dug was painful.

I'm not sure how long I had been without sleep. Though I found I could go without sleep longer than I had ever before imagined, it was there in the coral that I was vividly impressed with the reality of eventually coming to the end. At that point, even if you force yourself to stay awake, your body and mind will not function normally. Late in the progression of fatigue, you can stay awake by strength of will, but your reflexes and reaction time are desperately slowed.

As I dug at the coral, a Jap ran out of the bushes a few yards in front of me. My mind said "Jap! Jap! Shoot him!" Before I could make my body respond, the Jap had run across a little cleared area in front of me and was out of sight in the undergrowth beyond. I dropped the pick and fired into the bushes where I had last seen him, but I am sure to no avail. I was so tired that I could not make myself react quickly even when my life might well depend on it.

One classic example of the difference in values between a normal, peaceful life and the stress of battle happened on what I remember as the second or third day on Peleliu.

Norb Lamm and I were close buddies who had started out in the war together. As the Aussies would say, we were cobbers.[3] Norb was rather heavy-set and he sweated a lot on the long patrols. He was also thoughtful, kind, and a conscientious marine. He was from a well-off family in Webster Grove, Missouri, where his dad had a bottling works. Lamm had a girl back in Missouri who was engaged to him. He also had a brand-new black Plymouth convertible, with a white top, that was jacked up on blocks in the garage back home. He showed me a picture of it. I had a combination cigarette case and lighter he admired so much that I gave it to him.

On that day on Peleliu Lamm had drunk all his water, and he was obsessed with the idea of getting more. During one of the times that we stopped moving, Lamm began foraging in the bushes in an area on our flank. In a little while he came back with a Jap canteen about half-full of clean, cool water. The canteen was light brown and shaped rather oddly. I thought it looked a lot like a hot water bottle. Anyway, one of the boys talking to Lamm offered him two hundred bucks for the water in the canteen, something that in everyday life most people take for granted. All you do is go to a tap and run yourself a glassful. Lamm told him there wasn't enough money to buy it all, but he'd give the guy a drink for nothing, and he did.

I don't know whether Lamm shot the Jap or found him already dead. The important thing to Lamm, other than having the water to drink, was that the Jap's water was cool. That meant there was a source somewhere close. Lamm kept up a diligent search whenever time allowed, and he finally found the water. I can't recall exactly what it was — a well or a pond or what — but he took one of my canteens and filled it for me. I still had a little of it left when our supply units got water ashore to us.

Lamm was wounded a few days later. He was evacuated to New Caledonia and could have gone home. However, he chose to come back to his outfit. He was the leader of one of the squads in my section when we went to Okinawa.

Bob Miles, a rifleman buddy from Arkansas, said there was a thin line between sanity and insanity and that we learned to live on both sides of it. On about the third or fourth night, Miles and I were standing watch in the jungle between the airport and the village of Ngardololok, near the east coast of the island. He had a BAR and I had the machine gun. They sent us up a war dog and his keeper for sentry duty that night. Every once in a while the dog would stretch out and close his eyes. Bob would nudge the dog with his foot. The keeper got kind of pissed off and said the dog wasn't asleep and we should leave him alone. Maybe so, but we kept our own watch. We were glad when they left and never came back. That sure as hell was no place to count on somebody and find him not there.

On one of those first hectic days on Peleliu, days filled with hideous chaos, mutilation, and death, I learned to pray. I had a spiritual experience. (A similar phenomenon occurred on Okinawa that was more profound. More about that later.)

Certainly I had prayed before. My people were good folks who taught me to believe in God, so I had gone through the motions of praying. Even quite seriously and earnestly at times, as when my dear brother died. I was just a little boy then, and I felt the helplessness of mortals in the face of death, but in a quiet way. Even on earlier campaigns such as Talasea, when a rain of Jap mortars blew pieces of my fellow marines that stuck to my face and clothes, I had not been tested as on Peleliu. The many sleepless hours ran into days. They were filled with physical stress to the point of exhaustion and mental anguish that did, indeed, strain a man's sanity.

Battle, pitched battle, is extremely noisy. When the big stuff hits, artillery, mortars, and the like, it makes the earth shake and your ears ache. It splinters large trees like matchsticks and gouges great holes in the ground. It makes pitiful, unrecognizable remnants of what once were men's bodies, and it sometimes leaves nothing of the bodies, blows them completely away. You have to keep reminding yourself that you are still on the face of the earth. The inevitability of a mortar or artillery barrage was excruciating. There was nothing you could do about it, and you were completely at its mercy. Luck, or the grace of God, was all you could hope for, all that could save you. If you happened to be where a round was going to land you were SOL.

During a barrage of artillery between the airport and Ngardololok, I found out what Mother must have meant when she told me man's extremity was God's opportunity. I looked up at the air bursts to see how close they were. If they are nearly straight above you, you have a better chance of the shrapnel missing if you stand up by a tree, rather than lying down on the ground. God has always seemed to be "up" to me, and when I looked up at the air bursts I saw above them, alone in the sky, one little white cloud. I could almost hear my Grandmother Annie McNamara Ferguson telling me "God's in his heaven and all is well," as she had when I was a child in Nebraska and was frightened by thunder and lightning. As I watched the little cloud, I silently repeated the Lord's Prayer. It seemed so very definite to me that someone was listening to my prayer, and in the midst of all the hell around me, I felt exceeding peace.

In those first days on Peleliu we lost our CO. Regrettably, I am not sure of his name, and I haven't been able to find it in my research so far. I do remember, however, that he was a prime company commander. He was knowledgeable and efficient in his capacity. He was considerate of his men, and I remember him as one who often smiled. He treated his men not so much as subordinates but more like friends. By his demeanor he fostered allegiance and fidelity.

From somewhere in the chain of command, they sent us a temporary replacement. A highly ranked officer he was, poor fellow, and perhaps somewhere he deserved to be that rank. Perhaps as a recruiter, a judge advocate, or something of the kind, but not in a line company. I shudder whenever I think of him, and I am grateful to the corporal, my squad leader, who had the guts to tell the man, with necessary tact, to go fuck himself.

As it happened, when the officer arrived in our company area, he came directly to our gun crew. He had heard about the damage we had done the Japs the first night on Peleliu and wanted to visit with us. He appeared to be quite a pleasant and reasonable fellow. I imagine that he was an intelligent person as well. However, it very soon became evident that he was not endowed with the kind of experience that would make an efficient line company commander.

We had moved into a wooded, marshy area after crossing the barrenness of the airfield. Our advance had been halted by a Jap artillery piece in some hills above us and we were resting, waiting for the word on how to proceed. We were having an unordinarily amiable visit with the new officer when squad leader Charlie Smith saw the flashes of the muzzle blast of the Jap artillery, and from this sight he could nearly pinpoint its location. It was positioned in a small ravine on the side of a fairly prominent hill around two thousand yards in front of us. After Charlie drew our attention to the placement, we watched the ravine until the gun fired again. We could tell exactly where it was.

When the officer saw where the artillery piece must be, he told Charlie to have Miller and me set up our machine gun and fire on it.

Charlie first asked if he was serious. When the officer assured Charlie that he was indeed serious and repeated his request, Charlie began to argue against such an illogical course. The Jap gun was a big one — probably 105mm or larger — that was undoubtedly shielded. If we expended forty or fifty futile little .30-06 rounds against the steel shield two thousand yards away, there would be a sizable smoke signal rising from our location. The Jap gunners could then bore-sight their weapon on that smoke and eliminate us easily with one or two rounds.

Charlie Smith was brave. Like so many good marine noncoms, he was sometimes a little reckless with his own life, but he was never reckless with the lives of his men. I don't remember exactly what his words to the officer were. The gist of what he said was that he thought it was a bad, bad idea. However, if the officer was determined to carry out his idea, Charlie would have us set up the gun and get it sighted in, ready to fire. Then he would send the remaining three of us out of the vicinity to where we could watch the effects of what followed, and he and the officer would fire the machine gun at the Jap artillery. This put a different light on things.

The man was not as experienced as he should have been for the position he was in, but he was no dummy. He could see he had made a big mistake, and to his everlasting credit he didn't try to use his authority to ride it out. He backed up gracefully by asking Smith what he thought we should do. I have very proud memories of the way Charlie handled the situation.

He asked our sergeant, Utter, to help him assess the situation. Then we set our gun up on a good, solid base and sighted it in on the Jap position. Utter passed the word to our company headquarters to ask the naval gunfire liaison officer to come up as quickly as possible. In a matter of minutes he was there, looking down the sights of our gun. We visited with him as he checked the sighting and his maps. Soon he radioed his ship instructions on where to fire one round. I'm disappointed in myself that I can't remember the name of the ship. It was a cruiser lying thousands of yards off shore. The sailors manning the guns on that ship were something else. A whole lot of marines in my outfit wouldn't have made it without them.

When the first round fired by the cruiser hit the ground, it was a little to the left of the Jap gun position. The navy officer called corrections and asked for one more round. It landed to the right of the objective, about the same distance the first round had landed to the other side. They had thus straddled the position, and the navy man called that information to his ship. In the corps, the term for what they had done was "bracketing the target."

The Jap gun was on rails that ran back deep into a cave carved out of the coral hill. From their lofty position, they had a bird's-eye view of us and everything we did. Whenever we tried to advance, the Japs would run the artillery to the mouth of the cave and blow away marines with an efficiency seldom obtainable with artillery. When we stopped they would run the big gun back into the cave. Until Smith saw the flashes when it fired, we never knew exactly where the Japs were, and our searching counterartillery measures were futile.

But now the scene was set and a plan devised. We would feint an attack, tanks and all. The naval gunfire forward observer would watch for the Jap gun flash. When it fired he would immediately call for return fire to try to catch the gun exposed at the mouth of the cave.

It all went like clockwork. We started our attack and sure enough the

Japs ran the gun out, figuring on another turkey shoot. When we saw the first flash of the muzzle blast of the big Jap gun, I was close enough to the navy man to hear him tell the sailors on the cruiser to commence firing. They laid a salvo of five-inch rounds right into the Jap's crotch. The cruiser fired several more salvos. All of them were placed with uncanny accuracy. I was glad to see every one of them, but I am sure that they wouldn't all have been needed, for the first salvo was dead-on.

I stopped to see a corpsman and he put some very soothing salve on my burned hands. He wrapped some soft gauze bandages around and around my palms and fingers, and my hands felt good. The supply units had brought us up some freshwater. Charlie Smith and I split a can of meat and vegetable hash. When we moved out, the big enemy gun was silent. For a brief moment it felt like we might still be part of the human race.

Earlier campaigns had been spent in the jungles and in making landings against Japs hidden in protected positions, where they had huge advantages over us. We had been in a defensive position the first night on Peleliu, however, and as the Japs assaulted us we could see them. We could see our bullets tear into them. Moral or immoral, right or wrong, it had been very satisfying to get them out into the open, to be able to neutralize so many of them in such a short time. "Here, you little bastards, have a belly full of good ol' American steel." But now that was behind us. Once again it was the same old story: Run at them fast enough, or crawl at them low enough, so that they couldn't shoot all of us before some of us could shoot them.

At one point in our advance, I was manning the gun while Miller was eating. Our platoon leader, Lieutenant Wilcox, came up and stopped at our position. (In combat conditions it wasn't proper to address officers as "sir," or by stating their rank, because it might single them out for snipers or ambush. For this reason we all called Lieutenant Wilcox "Pappy.") He noticed my bandaged hands and asked me how they were. If all officers in the corps knew how many times their most casual consideration means so much to their men, I am sure they would take more time and make an effort to let their appreciation show. I told Pappy my hands would be all right before long. He put his arm around my shoulder and said, "Good man, Johnston, good man." It is one of my most pleasant memories of the corps.

I always liked Pappy. Later, in our rest area on Pavuvu, after we had left Peleliu, he'd bring a bottle to our tent in the enlisted men's area and we'd relive parts of the war. One time he showed up with tears in his eyes, and he told us it was the last time that he'd be joining us. The CO had forbidden him to fraternize with the men.

As we moved forward, northeast across the island, we came upon an area that was quite swampy. We found a narrow earth-filled grade that ran through the swamp. This is another of the places I have since revisited frequently in my dreams. I have no idea how long this causeway was, but I remember well how narrow. There were vehicle tracks on the surface but it was not wide enough for trucks to pass each other. Once in a while there would be a short, narrow grade extending off the main causeway at right angles into the swamp. At the end of one of the short joining grades, probably thirty or forty feet from the main causeway, there was a little filled area that had a grass shack on it.

As we advanced down the causeway we drew small arms fire. As we charged into this fire, we ran down the graded area a few yards at a time and then dropped down on the side of the hill for the protection it offered us. We brought fire to bear on suspect enemy positions and then tried to advance again. Once or twice we had called for fire support from our mortars and artillery and then had been able to continue our advance. One time when we stopped, I was close to the grade that ran to the grass shack. There was no door on the shack and I could see into it. On one of the posts near the doorway I could see a beautiful dagger hanging. Some Jap daggers, or short swords perhaps, were made so that the handle and scabbard looked almost like one piece — all the same hunk of metal — until you pulled the blade from the scabbard. The one in the shack was like that. It seemed to be bright white enamel with a gold (or at least gold-colored) design running through the white. For a moment I was sorely tempted to run down the few yards to the shack and grab it. Before I could make up my mind to act, the sniper fire began again and we started to move out. I had the thought that it had been just as well to leave it — the dagger might be mined anyway.

We had only gone a little way when I heard the muffled explosion behind us. I don't know who it was that got hurt or how many of them. They were not men from our company. They must not have been far behind us, though, for the word came up to us very quickly to be especially watchful for booby-traps. A marine had tripped one in the hut we had just passed.

The fight along the causeway had been intense for a while. It makes for vivid dreams, but we came to the end of it before I would have expected. The hard, dry ground widened out into a fairly pleasant area and we reached the ocean. We were on the opposite side of the island from our initial beachhead, north and east of where we had originally landed. We had secured the airfield and completely crossed the island, through the village of Ngardololok, to the beach on the other side. How we all hoped that we were through with it, but that was not to be. We had a saying in the old corps: Wish in one hand and shit in the other, and see which one gets full first. Such is the way the campaign was on Peleliu.

We were far from through at this point. We were fortunate, though, to have what I recall as a couple of days of comparative respite there on the beach. We patrolled the surrounding area but ran into only light resistance. The Japs tried to land reinforcements on the island around Purple Beach, south of us, but they were repulsed before they got to us.

When I remember some of the things I ate while I was in the field, I am not surprised that I ended up with intestinal parasites. On the beach near Ngardololok our site showed signs of recent human habitation, cleared areas and rocked walkways. A fine pair of very large, powerful binoculars was mounted on a pivoting stand. There were a few small huts, and next to one of them was some food, in the form of small oval-shaped cans with red labels. On the labels were blue pictures of salmon and a bunch of Jap writing. With my little GI can opener, I found one of the cans to be filled with fish heads. Not too appetizing, so I searched further.

On the floor of one of the huts I found a heap of loose rice that I put to immediate use. I filled my canteen cup about half full of water and shaved some of my D ration bar (chocolate) into it. Then I added the Jap rice to the mixture, just a little rice because I knew it would swell when heated. Then I built a fire and heated it all. Before I finished eating it, I noticed some of the rice moving. On closer inspection I found that quite a large part of the rice pile was maggots. That was one helluva chocolate pudding.

One day at the beach a marine tank came rumbling down the causeway into our area and parked there under a couple of palm trees. The crew bailed out laughing and talking, and ran to the front of the tank, where one of the tankers crawled out on the turret gun. When I went over to check it out, I saw that the end of the turret gun was splintered. It was quite a site. I figured they had tried to fire it when there was some obstruction in the barrel, but one of the crew told me a Jap shell had done the damage when it hit the end of the gun. I don't know the mechanics of tank operation, so maybe he was pulling my leg when he described the freak accident to me. He said that when the shell hit, the turret spun around like a top.

The guy who had crawled out on the gun on the beach was sawing away with a hacksaw at the barrel of the turret gun, trying to cut off the damaged part. I wondered if the explosion of a Jap shell wouldn't bend the entire barrel. In any case, I doubted whether they would ever get the damage cut off, or whether the gun would work even if they were successful. When I left, they were taking turns on the saw. I learned afterward that they not only finished the alteration but also used the gun again and it worked as well as ever.

When we left the beach on the east side of Peleliu, around September 21 or 22, we completely circled the island. We went back across the airfield and past the beach on the west side of the island, north of our initial beachhead. We started into the hills to take the objective that the First Regiment had assaulted before they pulled out of the hills. I understood that the Seventh Regiment was going to make an attempt to take it from the other side.

On our way we stopped near a captured Jap gun emplacement made of coconut logs, which the CO of the Second Battalion of the Seventh Marines was using as a command post. His battalion was up in the hills. His name was Berger and he was a lieutenant colonel.

I could plainly hear him talking to General Rupertus, commander of the First Marine Division, on the radio-phone. Major Gayle was there also. Presently, Gayle took the phone from Berger. Gayle gave Rupertus his impression of what was happening in the hills, and suggested a different course of action.

Berger took the phone back and said, "Now, General, I don't think Gayle is being fair about this."

Though they didn't give me a vote, I was on Berger's side. I was in hope that the general would give him a long, long time to work on the hills. I'd been on Peleliu long enough to know it was going to be a hellhole from beginning to end.

When we got to the other side of the island, we stopped at a position in the hills directly below some of the most rugged topography. It was in the proximity of the ridges that formed the southwestern part of the Umurbrogol Mountains.

The machine gunners in my outfit sometimes couldn't carry their guns and accompany the BAR men because the terrain was too rough for handling or using the guns efficiently. We would then leave the guns with someone to watch over them, and the rest of the machine gun personnel went with the rifles. So it was to be on this occasion, and our men went into the attack on the hills with the riflemen. I was left to guard the guns.

We had no idea what course of action to expect. When we first started to move, we hoped we were leaving the island. We could not imagine the First Regiment leaving if there was still strong resistance, so we figured we'd do some mop-up to secure their area and then we could leave also. After the guys had moved into the hills a little way from where I was left with the guns, I heard the sound of a strong firefight. I began to have an ominous foreboding of what was really left.

At about that time, down the little trail that led into the hills came a friend of mine named Paddy Doyle. He was a sharp guy, always clean himself and he cleaned his gear at the first chance. He was built strong and carried himself well, like the posters you see of marines. He was tough, too, when he needed to be, but he was more kindly than you might expect from his looks. He had been over there a long time. Though I didn't know him as well as some others, he was always considerate of me and I appreciated him for that.

My appreciation for him had been enhanced by something that happened one time when we were aboard a merchant marine ship, going to or coming from a blitz. On the ship were slatted deck houses. They were covered to keep things inside somewhat dry, but you could see into them through the spaces between the slats that made up the sides.

One day, some of us heard the tirade of a merchant marine petty officer coming from one of these deck shacks, as he vented his anger on a young seaman from the regular navy gun crew. We had noticed this joker before, this petty officer. I'm not sure of his race but he was dark-skinned, and he was mean. He was being extremely abusive in his reproach of the little sailor, and he went on at length. We had been sitting on the hatch cover close to the deck shack. After Paddy had listened to as much of that as he could take, he looked through the space between two of the slats and said to the merchant marine, "Say, Mister, what are you, black or white?"

There was a little latched door on the shack, almost like a gate. The merchant marine came charging out that door and hollered, "Who said that?" Paddy never said another word, but he hit the petty officer square in the face, so hard that the blood squirted. The merchant marine went sailing off the hatch cover and clear across the deck. All that kept him from going into the drink was the little rope railing they put on all those old Liberty troop ships. When he got his faculties back, he took off for the superstructure and that was the last we saw of him.

A little later our CO made an announcement over the ship's loudspeaker. He said that any further problems between his troops and the ship's personnel could be cause for disciplinary action.

At the time I was guarding the guns, Paddy was a squad leader. It was out of the norm to see him coming down the hillside path alone. When he got fairly close, we exchanged greetings and I asked him, "What's the dope, Paddy? Are we pulling out?"

"Hell no, we're not pulling out. It's a son of a bitch, Johnston. There's Japs in caves all over the damn place. We're liable to be here next year."

I wondered why Paddy was returning from the action, so I asked him, "Did you come back after me and the guns?"

"Naw. I got shot."

"The hell you did. Where?"

Paddy unbuttoned his dungaree jacket and pulled back both sides. Bandages were wrapped all the way around his chest, right up under his arms. There was a bright red spot starting to soak through the bandage just about in the middle of his chest. Pointing to the spot, he answered, "Right there."

"Good Lord, man, you gotta get something done about that. I can't leave these guns unwatched, but if you'll stay here I'll run down an ambulance or some stretcher bearers."

"Naw. It'll be OK. I can make it back up to the road. Good luck to you guys, Johnston."

He started off. As he walked away I could see a hole in the back of his jacket where the bullet must have come through. I called after him, "Yeah, good luck to you, too, Paddy."

He had certainly assessed the situation properly. It was a son of a bitch throughout the hills, for the full length of the island.

Along the beach, north of our initial beachhead, there was a very primitive-type road, just a wide trail, called the West Road. It ran on a narrow, flat strip of ground between the ocean and the abrupt coral hills, the sea cliffs. When our men came out of the hills where Doyle had been hit, we took the guns and started up West Road. We were trying to get to the north end of Peleliu, which was across a strait from another, smaller island, Ngesebus.

The Japs in the hills, having full view of West Road, could pick off anyone on the road by using direct (and quite short-range) small arms fire. Part of that road we called Dead Man's Curve. When we tried to advance up the road, the Jap rifle and machine-gun fire from the flanking hills was devastating. From West Road we attacked the Japs in their various positions, trying to neutralize their fire.

It was there that my friend Johnson from Texas and four other men started to run across an open area on the road. With typical deadly accuracy, the Japs shot four of the five in the head, including Johnson.

Because of the alphabetical nearness of our names, Johnson and I had always been assigned duties and stations close to one another. When we got overseas, he soon had command of a squad. He was savvy, strong, and gung ho.[4] I saw him every once in a while, and we always hailed one another and shot the shit if time allowed. I had run into him after Talasea and was grateful to see him alive. I had said, "Johnson! I wondered if you'd made it through." He had answered, "Don't worry, cobber. They haven't made the bullet with my name on it."

It was the first time I had heard that expression, and it had given me an odd feeling. I thought of it again, ironically and sadly, when I saw his body next to the roadway on Peleliu.

Following Johnson's attempt, we ran tanks up the road and turned them to fire into the hillside. As the tanks covered the area, an artillery outfit brought up a shielded 155MM rifle and fired point-blank into the hillside.

When they ceased firing, our infantry tried to advance on the road but the snipers were still there. Then we fired the tanks' guns into the hillside until infantry could close on the snipers' positions, in caves in the hillside. When the tanks ceased their support fire, the infantry charged the remaining few yards to the enemy positions. A BAR man stuck the barrel of his weapon into the small openings in the cave positions. He fired several clips into each position. Then a demolition man dropped satchel charges into the caves that blew some of the openings closed. A tank with a bulldozer blade covered them over. After that we could advance once again. When night came we stopped and set up perimeter defenses on the flat area. The Japs in the hills plastered us with artillery and mortars and sent infiltrators to penetrate our lines. In the morning we advanced again.

When we finally got through the area where Johnson was killed, we moved on, nearly to the end of the island, close to a phosphate plant. We then moved to our right flank to attack the hill complexes. We reached a saddle between two high points in a coral ridge. Toward nightfall Joe Lunsford and I crept and crawled up to the high point on our left and set up a night watch. The ridge was very narrow, only a yard or two wide, and it dropped off sharply on both sides. Sometime in the night we could hear Jap movement on the east side of the ridge. Soon Joe saw a Jap close to us near the top of the ridge, and Joe shot him in a firefight. We could hear the Jap falling down through the brush on the side of the ridge. In the morning there were bullet holes in the gear we had piled on the ridge to mask our silhouettes but Joe and I were unscathed.

We got through the hills at the far end of the island and started back on the south or east side of the hills to neutralize the pockets of resistance we had surrounded. Any map of Peleliu that shows the actions of the Fifth Regiment in the hills by means of arrows pointing in the direction of attack looks like a snapshot of an Indian battle: arrows going every which way — first in one direction, then in the other.

Typically, through all the high ground, we moved out over a ridge and caught automatic small arms fire. When we moved against the places from which we were taking casualties, we would take fire from a different direction. If the effort got too costly, we pulled out and attacked the pockets again from an entirely different direction. The results were always the same. Over the ridges and around the coral spines or high points, we would always draw more automatic small arms fire from many interlocking and overlapping lanes of fire. The place was like the catacombs, always impossible to figure where you were coming from and where you were going to, and toward the last we were attacking through the tombs of many young men, both Jap and American.

On one occasion, as we fought inch by inch through that rugged terrain, we crossed a little knob and came upon the remains of a bunch of Seventh Marine bodies, blackened and swollen from flame throwers cooking them. The flies and the birds and the maggots were working on them. It looked to be what was left of a platoon of good, young Marine Corps rifleman and machine gunners.

It was repulsive beyond imagination.

I am so grateful that Mother saved my letters. When my mind starts to bog down in confusion or sorrow as I write these words, I read some of the letters that I wrote home during that time. They bring back such vivid memories. It is very sad and I weep a lot, but I want to write the truth.

The next letter home is dated October 5, 1944. On the day the letter was postmarked, what was left of the Seventh Regiment pulled out of Peleliu's bloody hills. My mother's note on the back says "Rc'd Oct. 15th," so the mail was going out in pretty good shape. The letter was written on Jap paper obtained after a successful assault on one complex of hills. There is Jap printing in the margins of the pages that I would like to have translated.

> Dearest Mom and Dad,
>
> I am sitting on top of the highest hill on Peleliu.
>
> I am fairly certain this letter will reach you for I am entrusting it to what may remain of the squad when this is over. There are still three of us — Jimmy Miller, Joe Lunsford and myself.
>
> If you could do it easily I would like to have you write to Mrs. S. H. Lunsford, (Timberlake, North Carolina, Rt. 1) and tell her that I have lived with her son under conditions far more difficult than most people shall ever know. Tell her I have watched him closely in many ways and tell her she should love and cherish him for he is the salt of the earth. He is so courageous!
>
> He is always singing some old hillbilly song and they are beautiful. He sings one very often that is my favorite (he is at it now. It goes, "The rain is slowly, slowly falling, / Upon my window pane tonight, / And though your love is even colder, / I wonder where you are tonight.")
>
> I must close now. I want you to know that I am at peace with the Lord and all is still well.
>
> Jim

The Joe Lunsford of my letter had joined my unit on Pavuvu, after the New Britain campaign. He was a tall, willowy boy from North Carolina. It was soon obvious he had been raised by a good family who taught him the value of principles. Through the course of deep trials, we became as brothers.

To me, Joe epitomized the strength of the Marine Corps. Not the spit and shine, or the bullshit, but the part that got the job done. You never had to wonder about Joe. He was trustworthy, forthright, and open about everything. If you went into the jaws of hell, Joe would be with you, even without your asking. He would give me anything he had if I wanted it, and I the same with him.

I had also written in the letter about having had ill feelings about some "noncombatants". Not everyone, everywhere, had "total dedication to the war effort." (A bitch and her accomplice, for one, had rolled Frenchie in Dago.) We had some bull sessions about the high-paid defense workers who struck for more pay while the war was on and the true warriors were putting out so much for so little.

Very few people in the States really got very close to the war or understood what it was all about. It's not human nature to make yourself miserable with commiseration very long, even if you know what is happening. There is only one way to know what war is like and that is to be in the middle of it. Most people at home had too good a life to be genuinely concerned. I think of the old saying (Chinese I think): "One sore tooth in one's own head hurts more than a thousand dead in another country." I also think of what Ernie Pyle, the renowned war correspondent, wrote after he had returned to the States from the war in Europe and was at a party talking to some industrialist. After they had talked a while about his products, the economy, and such, the man asked Ernie what it was he didn't like about the war. According to his account, Ernie answered, "My God man, if you don't know, I could never tell you."

When my old friend Morgan E. Gilmour went home, before Peleliu, I gave him my folks' address and asked him to write them the "straight dope" when he got back to the States. Mother was very grateful to receive his letter. In a letter to me, he wrote, "You wouldn't believe what's going on here. Most of these people don't know there's a war, Jim. If I was back overseas I wouldn't raise a finger to save my own life, not if it would help these money grabbing bastards make a half-D."[5] Gil had been overseas too long. There he thought we were all in the thing together. When he got home he was sorely disillusioned. Damn few people had any idea what the war was like, and most didn't care to find out.

On the peak of a rim of hills at the north end of the island (or close to it), they stationed one gun, manned by Charlie, Jimmy, Joe, and me.

Meanwhile a bunch of our company, including a sergeant named Allison, went across the strait with the Third Battalion to make a landing on Ngesebus. All of them were fine men — Allison and the boys that were with him — but the best of men sometimes make big mistakes. Allison and his men did, and they were extremely fortunate that it didn't cost them their necks.

It happened that on Ngesebus they found a rather sizable store of sake, and when the island had been secured, they all got pretty tanked up on the wine. It was late dusk when they came back over to Peleliu. They came up along the little, very narrow coral ridge where we were and stopped a few yards from us. They were pretty booze-brave and careless. Worse than that, they were noisy. They made us jumpy. We had been very quiet when we had moved the gun up on the ridge position because we heard Japs in the caves a few yards below us, on both sides of the ridge. Knowing our situation Utter had brought us up a full case of grenades. It was a place to exercise extreme care, to minimize any sound that would expose your exact position.

But our tipsy buddies weren't having any of that behavior. Much to our dismay, they continued to drink and laugh and talk. Fortunately for them, we were between them and the Japs. The evening was still young when Charlie Smith, with his tommy gun, shot two Japs who had gotten so close to us as to rule out the use of grenades. Their bodies laid only a few steps from our foxholes.

Allison belligerently called out, "What the hell are you guys shootin' at?"

When no one answered, we could hear him stumbling along the ridge like a bull in the woods. When he got closer he asked, "Who did the shootin'?"

When he got close enough to us, he demanded again, "What the hell are you guys shootin' at?"

Smith pointed at the Jap bodies on the ledge and said, "Those guys right there."

You could barely hear Allison as he made his way back down the ridge and it was the last sound we heard from that direction for the rest of the night.

Charlie Smith was the kind of guy you knew when to dick around with and when not to. He was an easygoing guy that smiled a lot. He was a lot of fun to joke with but when he was serious, everybody was serious.

From that place on the ridge we worked back on the sides of the hills that were opposite the side of the island that we originally landed on. For days and nights and weeks, we assaulted the coral hills and caves, inch by inch, taking heavy casualties all the time. It got tedious. We got very little sleep.

As always in combat, even when we could lie down to rest for a few minutes, we had to try to sleep on the ground — in this case, the hard and sharply pointed spines of coral. We were usually so tired that we could in fact sleep on it, but when we got up our skin would look like the surface of a sponge because of the dents the coral had made in it. We usually had to rub the circulation back into those areas of our skin.

In the last days of September and the first weeks of October, the Fifth fought in many different places. We came to know some parts of the hills by nicknames, like the Five Sisters, Five Brothers, Baldy, the China Wall, Horseshoe Valley, Waddie, and others. Some were known only by the numbers that denoted their elevation. We took enough of the hills to make Dead Man's Curve on the West Road safe for travel. We secured Hill 140 and Baldy above Knob Three, where parts of the Seventh Regiment took so many casualties before they left us to join the First Regiment back on Pavuvu.

We moved south down the East Road, which ran through the hills on the east side of the island, and moved into position to make another assault in the hills. We had paused to rest a few minutes on the slopes of one of the ridges, and as I started to sit down I heard a strange sound — like a *whirrr!* I looked up and saw a blinding flash of light. The world spun and then it was very dark. From somewhere in the distance, I heard people ask, "What's his serial number?"

I tried to say my serial number but the haze I was in made me incoherent. Slowly consciousness ebbed back into my brain and I opened my eyes. The world was still a dark gray.

My God! Was I blind? No, I had fallen on my back when a piece of shrapnel hit me in the head, and the problem with my sight was that blood had run into my eye sockets. I rolled on my side and tried to wipe my eyes free of blood. The corpsman had covered my right eye with a bandage. Soon I could see light and images with the other eye. I had prayed that either I would see again or I would die. Things become very elemental in the corps. How much did you want to live? What would you rather sacrifice than die? To me, it was never a question as far as my eyes were concerned. If I had to be blind to live, I would rather have died.

When I recovered my bearings to the point of moving around, I started to walk back to the little medical tent we called a hospital, to get checked out. I caught a ride on a jeep for the end of the trek.

While I was in the hospital, I helped carry some of the newly arriving wounded, when I was able. One was belly-wounded — badly blown up. We put him on one of the tables, but no one came to take care of him. He asked me for a cigarette. I lit one and handed it to him. When he drew on the fag, smoke came out of the wounds below his rib cage. I drew a doctor's attention to the man: "Sir, I think someone should look after this boy. He's pretty bad."

The doctor's eyes lowered and he said, "I'm sorry, son. He's dead. He just doesn't realize it yet."

I've heard and read accounts of similar happenings reported by other people, but this account of mine is what *I* saw. I think of the Bible, Revelations 21: "And I, John, saw . . ." In this case I, Jim, saw. I held the guy's hand in mine. When I lit his cigarette, and watched the smoke drift out the holes in his body, it made a lasting impression on me. In a few minutes his eyes closed forever. I took the butt from between his dead fingers.

The first letter following the one written from the hill on Peleliu was written in the medical tent. Mother's note on the envelope says "Wounded — no date."

Dearest Mom and Dad,
    I am in the hospital. You will probably receive word that I have been wounded. Please believe me when I say it is only a

scratch. Of course I have no control over what will happen later, but as yet I am in A-1 condition. I am printing to save space. V-mail is all I have — am lucky to get that. I have received your letters right along — they are wonderful. Did you ever get the pictures? Tell Luke's Mom they were in his camera. Maybe they were like my watch.[6] I'm still on Peleliu. Will let you know along if I can. Keep your sweet chins up. We'll all pray for the best and all will be right. The old world will be peaceful again — so I must close. Tell Cornelia, E.P. and all "Hello." Give Gaylord my love.[7]

Jim

I was wounded in the afternoon of October 8 and went back to duty on the morning of October 11. The few men left of the Marine Corps contingent on Peleliu were not enough to do the jobs required, so I went back to my outfit, as did many others. My head was bandaged and still bleeding, and the vision in my right eye was still blurred. It never did clear completely, and only an eye examination after the war revealed the nature of the damage. I didn't write the folks any more about the wound. They would have worried too much.

The next letter was postmarked October 19, 1944.

Dearest Mom and Dad,

Well, it hasn't been long since I wrote to you and I have the opportunity to write again so here I am. My head is all healed up.

Mom, I didn't get any souvenirs this time. I could have had anything I wanted — sabres, pistols, flags, money or most anything you can think of but I just didn't have the heart to get them. There were so many of my buddies killed that I just didn't want any souvenirs. I don't want anything to remind me of the place.

We are resting now and there is not too much to worry about for a while. I would sure like to go home after this one but there are so many guys over here that have been here longer than I have that I don't count on it. If I don't make it [out] this time, it will be probably almost a year more. I will have sixteen months in a few days.

I must close before I use up all Joe's stationery. (Joe is singing in the rain and it is beautiful.)

God bless you 'till we meet again.

Jim

Soon after, we pulled off Peleliu and rode amphibs over to another little island close by, called Kongauru. Because it was closer to the big Jap complement on Babelthuap, we were wary of counterattacks from the north, but none came. We found a few Koreans the Japs had used as slave labor but that was about all. *Washing Machine Charlie*, a slow, light Jap aircraft came over a few afternoons and dropped one little bomb each time, but I don't think he ever hurt anything.

We stayed in one position there for a few days, giving me the opportunity to write home. That letter is postmarked October 20, 1944, and was pretty dull repetition except for a quote from an article in a magazine I found somewhere. The article stated, "It will be at least two years after Germany surrenders before Japan is defeated." I added, "That gives you a rather dark outlook. It is the truth, though. Most people at home think Japan will give up when Germany surrenders — Japan is just as strong as Germany! They will be harder to whip because of their geographical location — see if I'm not right!"

The next postmark is October 22. Dad had sent me two twenty-five-dollar money orders long ago, in case I ran short. In the letter I wrote, "First off, I just thought of something — those two twenty-five-dollar money orders you sent me. I have lost them, or rather the rain ruined them and I have my fears that they are too old for you to get your money back from them. I am sure sorry because that is a lot of money."

It was a month's pay for a marine private, it was probably the equivalent of the total cash I'd get from five or six months of paychecks, after insurance and bond allotments were deducted. In the letter I asked Mother what was wrong with Grandad. She must have written that he was ailing. I wrote, "I wouldn't look for many letters from Gilmour. It is a strain on him to write. He very seldom wrote to his own people — you can feel honored."

My letter continued,

Charlie Smith has been over here twenty-nine months, Jimmy Miller two years today. Jim and Charlie should be going home soon. Jim lives at Lexington, Ky., and Charlie at Lawrenceburg, Tenn., about 150 miles from home. Either one or both of them are liable to come visit you. They are great guys and worthy of what you can do for them if they should happen to come see you. Jim is liable to be a little bashful and maybe Charlie, too, but you will know how to handle them, talk to them etc., I know.

God bless you always and I'll love you 'til then.

Jim

In the few days after that, we went back to Peleliu and boarded transports to leave the son of a bitch for good. Even after weeks of taking the bloody, fucking coral hills a few feet at a time, there was still a pocket of resistance about three hundred yards wide and six hundred yards long that would cause suffering for elements of the poor old Wildcats (the army's Eighty-first Infantry Division, which relieved us). As we sailed away I watched until the battle-blackened ridges and peaks of Peleliu were out of sight and silently reaffirmed that I never wanted to see that place again.

There are many things to remember about the Palaus, but very few of them are pleasant. The Peleliu campaign is regarded by most strategists as a terribly expensive mistake, unquestionably costing more than it was worth. From what information is available to me, I would say that is probably true. There are many reasons to doubt if it was worth anything in terms of the big picture. I hear that there are questions in high places about the judgment of the CO, about his decision to stay at the costly endeavor as long as he did. My thought is that though Peleliu was a costly mistake and a bad idea from the beginning, what was the general supposed to do? Should he get great numbers of his men killed and maimed trying to finish the job someone gave him? Or should he pull out leaving some enemy ground untaken? If he pulled out, he would be saving a lot of young marines, but he would most assuredly be getting his own ass canned in the process. Sometimes being a general couldn't have been easy, either.

Tennyson wrote, "Theirs not to reason why, / Theirs but to do and die: / Into the valley of Death . . . Rode the six hundred." But with us, it wasn't into the valley that we had ridden. It was on to the atoll. And it wasn't six hundred casualties, it was well over six thousand, in the First Marine Division alone. I don't know how many casualties the army had, but I know they suffered heavy losses. In William Manchester's book *Goodbye, Darkness*, he wrote of visiting Peleliu many years after the war. He took a photo of the monument an army unit had built there in honor of their fallen comrades. The monument was seemingly uncared for, neglected, and decomposing.

I have heard recently that someone later raised a monument to the marines on Peleliu. I think that was a bad idea. If I was going to put up a monument to the boys who fought and died on Peleliu, I would put it on the lawn in front of the White House in Washington DC.

I don't relish the idea of the care the Jap visitors will give any American marine remembrance on Peleliu — and I'm too far away to do anything about it.

I built my memorial to my friends in a poem I sent to Mother in a letter dated December 21, 1944:

COVERED WITH SAND
In the hills of Peleliu,
where the blood and guts were strewn
Around in little piles that once were men,
We found which boys were strongest
and which ones could last the longest,
And we watched the strongest dyin'
now and then.
'Cause there was no way of shirkin'
from the hell that we found lurkin'
Behind each bush and every little rise.
The yella bastards shot
and some gyrene likely got
A bullet, like as not between the eyes.
So we laughed at Japs that fell

and went on their way to hell
With a belly full of copper-coated lead.
And we wished with every one
that the whole damn war was done,
And every Nip that ever lived was dead.
When we got so sick of tryin'
that we didn't care for dyin',
We'd try to cheer each other up and say,
"Get a hold on yourself, Buddy —
the whole old world ain't bloody,
There'll be peace and quiet
come again some day."
So we played the gory game
in a way that did us fame,
Knowing that with every passin' day
There'd be unlucky ones,
some other Mothers' sons
That had the price of precious life to pay.
And we prayed for them that stayed
in the holes where they were laid.
They'll never go a-marchin' to the band.
And the tears came to our eyes
when we watched the crosses rise
Where we'd laid them in
and covered them with sand.

I had written Mother that I had made a poem of sorts, and she asked me to send it to her. I apologized to her for my ineptness as a poet but hoped that what the little poem lacked in structure would be tempered by my depth of sincerity.

Over the years I have read accounts of the battle for Peleliu that seemed to disparage the work of the Fifth during that campaign. This has always troubled me greatly, for I know them to be far from the truth. The First and Seventh Regiments fought bravely and well, and they suffered heavy losses, to be sure. But the Fifth remained in the struggle for many days after both of those units had pulled out of the fighting, and it was responsible for securing much of the island. The Fifth fought bravely and well, also — first in securing its objectives during the initial days of the campaign, and later against enemy positions that the other units had failed to take.

It, too, suffered heavy losses. When the riflemen and machine gunners of E-2-5 came out of Peleliu's hills, they mustered in a formation to load out and leave. As Utter counted the officers and men there, the tears rolled down his cheeks. Among those mustered were several casualties (including Bob Miles, Wiley Brown, Charlie Smith, and me) who had gone back briefly to our battalion aid station to get patched up, and then had returned to duty. Because I don't know how many, I can't be certain of our exact overall casualty count. Even counting the wounded that had returned, many more were gone than were remaining. To discredit the efforts of the Fifth on Peleliu does more than a disservice to those of us who survived. It sullies the memory of the many Fifth Marines who died in that godforsaken place.

When infantry units loaded on transport ships to go into battle, the holds of the ships were generally bulging at the seams with personnel. We slept in bunks stacked five deep, in areas of floor space barely large enough for a man to lie down. We always felt squeezed, everywhere we went. When we boarded ship to leave Peleliu, there was more than enough room for us. Stacks and stacks of bunks were empty. There was plenty of chow for everyone, meaning no chow line at all. It was almost lonesome.

Peleliu may have been a mistake, but I learned many things there on a personal level and even though most of them weren't worth what they cost, at least they were enlightening.

Included in Edwin Markham's anthology of the world's greatest poetry are selections from the work of Siegfried Sassoon. In his comments, Markham quotes from the soldier-poet Robert Nichols's preface to Sassoon's "Counter Attack." Nichols wrote, "Let no one ever say one word countenancing war. It is dangerous even to speak of how here and there the individual may gain some hardship of soul by it. For war is hell, and those who institute it are criminals. Was there even anything to be said for it, it should not be said; for its spiritual disasters far outweigh any of its advantages.

There is no question about the truth of that statement, but since I had to live the experience of war, I am going to glean from it what I can.

For me the corps would go on as it began — a series of extremes — until the end of my association with it. From the heights to the depths — happiness and sorrow, pride and shame, love and hate. There was no happy medium. Everything was intensified, even the boredom.

We went back to Pavuvu, back to the same company areas and squad tents we had left when we headed for the Palaus. Empty spaces all over the place. At least we didn't have to build a dry place to sleep again. As much of a shithouse as Pavuvu was, it was heaven compared with where we'd been. It almost felt like home.

7. *Return to Pavuvu*

WHEN I FIRST JOINED the First Division it consisted almost entirely of old salts — combat veterans — who looked upon me, the new recruit, with distrust and disdain. It was seldom that they would talk freely to me. However, they would sometimes talk openly and candidly to one another in my presence. I was rather surprised at the bitterness and lack of appreciation that, without exception, they all evidenced for medals for valor. Strangely, it seemed the more prestigious the medal, the more cynical they were toward it and its recipient. At the time, I wondered if jealousy prompted them, but the more I was exposed to the war, the more I realized how warranted their opinion was.

On Peleliu it was graphically proven to me that the awarding of medals for valor (and, as with the Medal of Honor, the accompanying hugh benefits) is an unqualified miscarriage of justice and a spurious practice. It implies that men with medals for valor are valorous and men without them are not. Nothing could be further from the truth. No man, or group of men, can make awards for valor with any degree of consistency or regard for worthiness. Everyone with any real experience in war realizes that fact. To use a system that is so grossly unjust is a flaw in the character of a society that professes to revere honesty and equity. Most regrettably, like the sirens that lured the sailors to destruction on the rocks, the system creates a pretense of honor and adventure and heroics to which conscientious youths will be naturally drawn. Thus by this fraud do we teach our children and the generations of the future.

Perhaps the worst inequity of all is the awarding of the most prestigious medals to short-timers — men who have been in combat only a brief period. They haven't been in the fray long enough to learn what bravery is. After a year or two of watching great numbers of their friends blown to hell, then what they do may no longer be ignorant foolhardiness. Even when given to men of more experience, there are great inequities in the awards, especially among men from different types of outfits. I have read many of the texts for awards of the Medal of Honor. Some of the medals were given to men whose units were not often involved with the intense struggle of combat that was so commonplace for the rifle companies. Had the recipients been in the infantry, their deeds would hardly have been noticed.

Day after day I have watched countless line company marines and infantry soldiers commit deeds of great courage and sacrifice and receive nothing for their efforts. To them it is their everyday job. Even among the front line fighters, the disparity between the deeds for which some of the Medals of Honor were given, and many more deserving deeds for which nothing was given, is enormous. After you have advanced through the bodies of four or five waves of marines on more than one occasion, you develop a very intense respect for them — not any of them specifically, but for them all.

When I write bitter condemnation of our practice of awarding medals for valor, I do so without malice toward the recipients of the awards. I simply say what I have said in whole-hearted support of the truth.

It may seem odd, but several men who made it through Peleliu committed suicide after we got back to Pavuvu. I always feel bad when I think of the guys that gave up on the world and killed themselves there. I don't blame them and I can understand it, but it still makes me feel bad.

A few more things broke up the norm on Pavuvu this time, besides the crack-ups killing themselves. Though I have heard quite a bit of discussion about the practice during some other wars, I never saw or heard of anyone intentionally fragging,[1] or killing, any of our own men in combat. If you did, you might be taking out someone who could have saved your life later, had you left him alone.

But something bizarre of this nature happened on Pavuvu. One day we heard small arms fire not too far away, which was unusual. There wasn't supposed to be any firing at that time. There was no enemy within miles. We got scuttlebutt about what had happened, but I never repeated it, not until after the war. One of my old schoolmates, who was on a small, interisland craft in the Russells, asked me what had happened to the officer whose corpse they took off Pavuvu. The body was pretty badly shot up.

I told my friend that, according to the scuttlebutt I got, there had been an NCO who had a lot of time in the islands and was on the list to go home before the next campaign. He would stay in his tent when chow call sounded and wait for the line at the mess hall to dwindle. Then he would take a shortcut across the corner of officers' country to save a long walk around, by road. The officer in question caught him doing that and, as punishment, took him off the list to go home. The sergeant then got his tommy gun, went to the officer's tent, said, "Mister, I'm the last man you'll ever foul up," and riddled the guy with .45 slugs.

I don't know what happened to the sergeant. They moved him out of there pretty quick. Whatever they did with him probably didn't beat him out of much. If he was off the list to go home, he'd have hit Okinawa with us as a rifle squad leader. He'd have had a good chance of living in misery for a few more weeks, or months, and dying anyway, especially since he would have been shitlisted.

For a long time I sort of got a kick out of that story, but the older I get, the more it seems to be a sad story, too.

Something else was new on Pavuvu. I don't know under what pretense they were there, but some women were encamped in a remote, restricted area. The word was passed that with certain pay-offs you could buy a few minutes of their company, for an additional price. I could never figure how a girl could undergo that kind of exposure without spreading a lot of disease, so I wasn't a prospect, but I got a laugh out of it, anyway. At the quoted price, after my allotments and premium were taken out of my pay, it would have taken me about two years of saving all the cash I got to buy a girl's company one time.

Music was always a very meaningful part of my life. I was never accomplished at it, as a singer or pianist, or in any other way. Still, I don't think anyone ever had a more profound appreciation of it than I. From my earliest recollection, I loved music of most any kind.

On the islands where we found ourselves, there was almost no music at all. Except for Bob Hope's troop and an occasional song out of one of my buddies, I hadn't heard any since we left Australia. Then, during our second stop on Pavuvu, an army entertainment group put on a show for us that was superb. They had an orchestra that was strictly first-class and a soldier-vocalist with them. When he came on stage, he said that his name, "oddly enough, is strange — Michael Strange." When Michael Strange sang Cole Porter's "Begin the Beguine," for a little while I felt like I was back in the real world.

Throughout my life certain songs have been reminiscent of certain times and places, I seldom hear "Begin the Beguine" that I don't sigh at thoughts of a tropical eve in a coconut grove in the Russell Islands long, long ago.

My buddy George Hartley kept me out of trouble, again, on Pavuvu. We were swimming off the docks, where there were also a bunch of other guys. We were diving off the boom of a crane that the CBs had parked on the docks. A couple of MPs (Military Police) came along and gave us the word that what we were doing was forbidden. They also informed us that the division was still needing line company replacements. This was, of course, a very thinly veiled threat. Everybody there but Hartley and me pulled on their dungarees and left. When the MPs asked us our outfit, we said, "E-2-5. Get us a transfer to Mare Island if you can."[2]

Of course we didn't mean that. It would have been a lot safer duty, but it would also have been a disgrace. However, the MPs didn't know the implications for us. They also failed to realize that no line company CO was going to transfer some of his combat-experienced people back to a stateside prison just because they had been swimming in the wrong place. So we went on diving off the boom. It was a big one, very high. I'd go up about a fourth of the way and jump off, but Hartley would go clear to the top and dive. He was very, very adept at diving and it was fun to watch him.

Shortly after the MPs left, Hartley climbed up the boom, but instead of diving as usual he turned around and scuttled down. When I asked him what was wrong he said, "Come here."

I went with him to the edge of the dock. "Look," he said, pointing into the water. I saw only a very ordinary sized fish, then another and another.

I asked Hartley, "Those aren't sharks, are they?"

"Hell, no, they're not sharks. They're barracuda. Let's get the fuck out of here."

All the way back to our tent area he told me stories about barracuda off Florida, where he came from. I was lucky and grateful to have a buddy who had so much experience, or I would have undoubtedly wound up fish bait in the bay off one of the Russell Islands.

On December 7, 1944, while on Pavuvu, waiting for replacements to fill the voids left by Peleliu and new gear needed for the Okinawa invasion, I wrote:

> Dearest Mom and Dad,
>
> It has been quite a while since I wrote to you folks. I hope you aren't worrying. It is just that my boys keep me quite busy. I am in charge of two squads and it is quite a job seeing that they get this and that and learn all they should. It is about like having a big family. They are a good bunch of boys, though, and someone has to look out for them (so it might as well be me). Joe is one of the squad leaders and I don't have any trouble with him.[3] He does what I tell him, first because he likes me, and second because it is his duty.
>
> I am doing a Sgt's job and if all goes well I may be rated to Corporal soon (two or three months).[4] It is hard to get rates because [in the corps] every outfit is allotted only so many rates and if there are not enough to go around it is just "tough." I don't count on anything, however.
>
> This is December seventh. Do you remember three years ago today? We were riding home in the car and we had heard all about Pearl Harbor. Somewhere between McCook and Wauneta we heard La Paloma [on the radio] and, Dad, you said, "Son, we

may be separated many miles some of these days but wherever you are and no matter how far separated we are when you hear that song, think of your old Dad."

Three years have passed since that day and two of them we have been separated these thousands of miles. I don't have much opportunity to hear that piece. Most of the time I can't even hear any music and when I can hear some, I can't request what I want; but, Pop, right now I'm hearing La Paloma, and do you know why? — because I'm whistling it.

I guess you know I'm really thinking of home — Christmas and all. In six days I'll be twenty-two.

Not much more to say except all's well and I'm happy and wishing you a Merry Christmas.

Jim

At twenty-one, I was the oldest guy in the section, except old man Wiley Brown, who was twenty-seven. He led one of the squads under my command. He aggravated me sometimes because of his constant bitching that I favored Joe's squad, but he was a good man and a good friend. He really liked booze and I most always let him have the rare beer ration I got. He insisted on paying me for it so he didn't feel beholden to mc. That was a joke because there was nothing there I wanted that I could buy with the money. I'd let him have the beer and pay me for it, anyway, to keep him happy. On the rare occasions that I gave the beer to anyone else, Wiley would damn near cry. He had been around a lot in civilian life, in some tough places. I learned a lot from him.

On December 26, 1944, still on Pavuvu, I wrote:

Dearest Mom and Dad,

Well folks I wrote to you yesterday but am writing a lot now whenever I have time in view of the day when I will again be unable to write. It is such a pleasure when I have a lot of time to sit down and write like I was talking to you.

I am very proud that I am a corporal. Also, I am doing a Sgt's job now and if I'm good enough at it I may make Sgt. before too long. Of course, as always, I count on nothing and so am not disappointed.

Dad, I know you refused to be rated in the army but here it is different. Here, as everywhere, experience is very valuable — I should say it is even more valuable here than most anywhere else because here you are dealing definitely with life and death. It is not only a man's privilege but his duty to put his extremely valuable experience to use by accepting the responsibilities and faith thus placed in him. You always taught me, Dad, (and I believe I will always follow it) to do the best I can wherever I am. I asked for this job and I'm proud of it. Our job is a hard and terrible one but our cause is just and our hearts are free. You can rest assured that I will do my utmost to take care of the men I have. I will do the best I can in their behalf.

I'll write again soon.

Jim

I had begun to feel the weight of the lives for which I was responsible — a weight that would soon become much heavier.

Sometimes a feeling comes over me that is so much the same as something felt before. It is akin to déjà vu but concerns a philosophy or emotion rather than a sight or place. There is an odd parallel between that time in my life and the present.

As I write this, I am rapidly becoming one of the "old timers." Mom and Dad are gone, along with most everyone else with more experience that I looked to for advice or guidance. I feel now almost exactly the way I felt when we came off Peleliu and were getting ready to go in on Okinawa.

Everyone who had been in front of me in my unit was dead or gone. It seemed like, almost at once, there was no one there who was more experienced or knowledgeable than I. There was no one to lean on for help. Wherever I looked, someone was looking back at me.

As a consequence, you may notice that I don't describe some of the men in my outfit on Okinawa as thoroughly as the men before them. It isn't that I have any less regard for them, only that so many of the men were new, and we had little shared experience. From Peleliu on, the war killed or maimed them so fast that we simply weren't together long enough for me to get to know them as well as the marines I had begun with.

I have heard a lot of conjecture, recently, about whether the United States should have dropped the atomic bomb on Japan, and I am convinced that a large part of our society has the wrong outlook on war. War is not a game to play by rules. In my judgment, if you must go to war and send your young men to some far-off hellhole to be slaughtered, then *anything goes*.

The bomb put an end to the Japanese thinking that they could barter better peace terms by killing as many of us as possible wherever we attacked them. How much more desirable it would seem to me for us to have pulled all our forces off the islands during the last few days the A-bomb was being developed, then to drop enough bombs on those islands to lower their highest elevations to a few feet below the surface of the Pacific Ocean. I am deathly serious when I say that if I could have done so, I would have blown Okinawa and all the sons of bitches on it into the sea. I wouldn't have hesitated to do the same thing to Japan.

Thousands of good young American servicemen died in the last days of the war, on the threshhold of the atomic age. Had it been handled differently, those faithful, sacrificing young American men might have come home to their families instead of making so many corners of Oriental fields forever American.

I guess it doesn't make much difference what I think in that regard, anyway. There's no doubt the movers and shakers would pay little attention to how I think we should handle such things.

But that wasn't the case with two squads of marines when we left Pavuvu for the last time and headed for Okinawa. Then, a bunch of young guys were looking to me to show them the way to make it through, and I was only praying I could.

8. Okinawa: The Last Invasion

THERE WERE SOME colorful and meaningful terms — idiomatic expressions — in the old corps. Some of them reminded me a great deal of slang expressions the country folks in Kentucky, my people, used to describe things. Kentucky jargon such as "there's a dead cat on the line" and "he could see the weeds partin'." They often conveyed thoughts and described conditions better than the most sophisticated speech.

Typical of the corps terms were "the thousand-yard look" and "the bulkhead stares," both used to describe the blank look that could come over a man pushed to his physical and emotional ends.

One term was, perhaps, more significant than all the rest. That term was "Asiatic." That tag went on a marine when he began to lose his hold on normal values, when he began to reconcile himself to the fact that he was no longer a human being but was now a marine, and that he would probably live and die as such, never to go home to life as it had been.

I would never have believed it would happen to me, but going to Okinawa I realized that, while I wasn't watching, I had become, at last, like all the rest of the old corps. I was Asiatic. I thought of the old verse "I knew a lad who went to sea / and left the land behind him. / I knew him well — the lad was me / and now I cannot find him."

One of the last letters I wrote home before we hit Okinawa, though undated, is postmarked on a day shortly before the invasion began. The last letters became increasingly more "cover-up" or "smooth-over" jobs than the earlier ones had been. I was trying to prepare the folks, as I had myself, to accept the fact that I had very little chance of coming home alive. Of course, hope springs eternal. When I was a child and traveled places with the folks, they often sang the old hymn "Whispering Hope." They sang in harmony and the hymn came to my mind often in those troubled times. Hope tends to grow stronger in greater adversity, though eventually you realize that your hope disregards what you believe is probable.

Dearest Mom and Dad,

I am just now getting the letters you sent during the time a short while ago that I could not write to you. You write of being anxious. I surely hope that by this time you have received some letters from me after the lapse. I am very sorry about that, but there is nothing I can do about it. However, I wish you would never get anxious because sometimes I am where I just can't write. You can rest assured that as long as I'm kicking I'll keep writing once in a while when I can. Of course there are a lot of deuces in the deck we play with over here and every body has to draw. If the deuce comes up then you drop out of the game. Then no more "through a glass darkly." If the deuce doesn't show, then precious people, I shall see you once more in the light of the world — so don't worry!

My friend Jack French and I were talking of war. You know, to say there is no fear of death in battle is foolish. Death is too prevalent for one to be unmindful of it. But the dread is not of death itself. It is rather an apprehension — an acknowledgment of the fact that if you die you will not know the pleasures of this world as it is at home. Oh! to see the folks — and snow and city lights and girls and old friends and new ones — and the blessed hills of home. Oh! to eat Mom's wonderful cooking and to drink that clear cool water — and a glass of milk!

On these pages I have drawn my heart and showed the little things, and the great ones, that haunt its deepest corners. So I'll say good-night — and we will see what we will see.

Jim

Each of the battles had an air of dramatic historical significance, both as they were forthcoming and as they transpired. Having avidly read the history of many battles, I knew that each of the names of those in which I would participate would later have special significance, both to me and to the history of the world. All through the war I was aware of that thought, but it lay almost idle in the back of my mind until the last campaign. When we started for Okinawa, the island was so close to Japan that I was acutely aware that we were making deep tracks in the history of the world, civilized or uncivilized.

I thought of the knights of old, engaged in mortal combat for their principles and high ideals, and it was difficult for me to realize that I had joined their ranks. It would probably cost me my neck, but I guessed whatever it cost it was worth. I also thought of young Julius Caesar as a front-line warrior, and how high the odds were against his living long enough to become the leader he later became. I realized that he and I had faced a common peril.

Again I was struck with conflicting emotions. I felt a real joy. I was grateful for the opportunity to be there, to be a part of the making of history, and I had an appreciation of myself for the strength of mind and body that it took to carry the load. But I was also sickened by contemplation of the morbid dread that always prefaced the coming of the maelstrom of battle.

When I begin to try to recount the Okinawa experience, I am nearly overwhelmed with emotion. I know this will not be easy, I still feel the feathers in my guts. Still, as the artist tries to paint the picture his mind sees, I will try to tell with words what I felt. Imagine, for a moment, that it is March 31, 1945.

It is night, black night aboard a huge, flat-bottomed LST (Landing Ship Tank) somewhere in the Pacific. Through the darkness, heavy and tight upon us, we wallow on toward the war.

I pace the deck for a little while, then go below to rest. I need sleep for strength to face tomorrow. But sleep will not come. Back up on deck I watch the phosphorus glow where the big ship's bulk breaks the ocean's surface and I think long thoughts.

At sunrise I will lead my men ashore against the hostile forces waiting there. We will be the first assault wave. Between us and the enemy there will be no buffer.

I have lived through many months of war, war of various kinds, sometimes down jungle paths and sometimes through the jungle where there were no paths. In support of the first assault waves, I have gone ashore to dodge among what is left of the men and machines of those waves. By some fate I cannot understand, I have lived to filter inland, there to charge some island's muddy mountains or to storm the battle-blackened coral peaks and caves, always threading my way through the bodies of men as good as or better than I. Somehow, in the course of days, I have always before reached the respite of the battles' ends.

Now the task awaiting us leaves little chance of survival. The shoreline we face is a sea wall rising about thirty feet abruptly from the water's edge in all but one place. That place is perhaps forty yards wide and is comparatively flat. Huge gun emplacements line its sides. This is our objective. We must try to secure the flat ground so the tanks and supplies can be landed there. All the defenses the enemy can muster — artillery, mortars, and machine guns — will concentrate their fire on that strategic forty yards. How in the world can a man live through such a place? I will not think specifically of death, but in my heart I know.

In the morning I must try to be an example for my men. Make sure the guns are working well and each man has grenades and ammo.

Throughout the night I seek for strength untapped. Fail not, man, fail not now! I check the gear again. I must be ready, I must concentrate on my job! If we get ashore, try to set the guns where you can bring their fire to bear on the resistance.

When I look at the faces of the young men who will be following me, who will do what I ask until their last breath, I feel a woeful, empty loneliness. Our officers have made no pretense about our part of the assault. Everyone expects E Company to be literally destroyed. We will have served our purpose if we can neutralize enough of the beach defenses to allow the unit behind us to get through.

When I had read of the futile and disastrous Confederate assaults on the defenses at Gettysburg, and the pitiful waste of the courageous Union troops in the assaults on Marye's Heights at Fredericksburg, I had felt horror and sorrow so deep it almost choked me.

I felt nearly the same intense admiration and commiseration whenever I read about the Charge of the Light Brigade at Balaclava and about the marines of my own outfit at Belleau Wood. How could men put other men in such places, or let themselves be put in such? And yet, here I was, charging on the way to almost certain extinction. It was the corps's way, do it or die trying.

The big ship has changed speed, so we must be nearly in position. The island we will assault lies between us and the sun. The first grey fingers of light, those that come before the pink, show in the east. Dawn is coming soon, too soon. No, not too soon, not soon enough. At least it won't be long before we know. Mother Mary smile on me, on us. It will surely be a miracle if any of us get across the beach.

Compared with the last islands we had been on — Pavuvu and Peleliu — Okinawa was pretty large. It was 454 square miles in area, a little over one-third the size of the state of Rhode Island. It was nearly seventy miles long and varied in width from two to almost twenty miles.

Naha, the principal city on the island, was on its west coast, and overlooked the East China Sea. The mean Fahrenheit temperature at Naha was sixty degrees in January and eighty-two in July. When we first arrived, the nights would drop to between forty and fifty degrees and later in the campaign the daytime temperatures neared ninety degrees.

The island had been inhabited for centuries and was badly overpopulated. All the available land was farmed in small patches. There were no jungles and the few trees growing were small evergreens. Okinawa was comparatively flat overall, gently rolling hills with some steep ridges and deep ravines. From a few high places you could see for miles in each direction. It was located 350 miles from the Japanese home island of Kyushu.

Those of us who were able to, ate what we could of an extra-special morning chow that the navy fixed for us. Then, after all the usual fuck-around of getting ready, we boarded the little landing craft that would take us in. There was the necessary milling around getting our organization formed. Then, on signal, all the little craft turned abreast and headed for the beach.

Our navy was laying down a tremendous barrage in front of us. In spite of the fanatical Jap air attacks on them, our navy maintained support until we were too close to shore for them to continue.

On the way in, something happened that was a huge morale boost to me then and has been an inspiration to me throughout the many years since.

As we passed the last of the navy support vessels, the one closest to shore, I looked up at the sailors on deck firing close-support rockets. As we passed, they fired the last rounds they could before we landed. I happened to be watching one gun crew directly. They were close to us as we passed. When they ceased firing one of the sailors turned toward us from his tubes. I don't suppose he could tell one of us from the bunch, but it seemed he was looking right at me. He raised his right arm high above his head with his first two fingers in a V, for victory. He could see where we were going. He had done the best he could for us and now he was sending his spirit with us. No service-rivalry bullshit there, only a team of Americans. I'll never forget the sight of that little sailor.

Because we knew of the gun emplacements straddling the narrow area in which we were to land, our plan was to run our machine gun squads out of the boats in the lead elements and set up immediately to bring all the firepower we could to bear against the emplacements.

When we passed the last support vessels, we started across the million miles that were the remaining few hundred yards to the beach. I felt the fearsome, awesome, exhilarating thrill of expectancy. For a moment, just before we landed, I remembered the bodies of the first waves of marines on Peleliu and how they had looked when we landed an hour or so behind them. I wondered what we would look like to the waves that would come behind us.

An amphibious assault requires a concentrated and continuous propulsion of force, so initiated and maintained that it will overcome that which opposes it, regardless of the strength of the defense, regardless of the cost in casualties.

When we hit the beach and the ramp came down, I took off ahead of my squads to try to find a likely place to set up the guns, a place we would have a field of fire that included the Jap gun emplacements.

Once you have been knocked silly from steel hitting you in the head, you have a fairly vivid imagination of what can happen. As I stumbled across the rocks on the beach, I anticipated the impact of bullets ripping into my body. It was an incredibly strange sensation.

When I had gone in a few yards, I could plainly see the ports from which their guns should have been firing, but there was no fire. So I kept moving toward their emplacements on the left. I had a tommy gun and several grenades. We seldom stopped an advance until we were forced to do so, especially on the beaches, so instead of stopping to set up the guns, we moved on in. I guess I thought I might get to the pillbox and dump some grenades through the gun ports before they got me. I don't know just how I expected to do that, unless the Japs were all asleep or blind or dead. While running across open ground at an enemy who has machine guns and artillery in concrete pillboxes, you don't stop to rationalize a great deal or you lose your enthusiasm.

To our great good fortune, the Japs had not manned the pillboxes! We got to them in a hurry and passed right on by. We took up normal attack formations and moved inland quickly. Beyond our wildest hopes and dreams, in an hour our beachhead was several hundred yards deep and growing by the minute.

Everyone was jubilant, absolutely overjoyed. As I have said, no one had tried to hide the truth from me. We were expected to be expended, and I had been completely candid with my men. We had resolved that we would go as far as we could, so that someone behind us could finish the job. When we got past the beach, it was as though we had been granted a pardon from the death sentence. It was sweet, however short-lived.

For many of my friends, it was only a reprieve. They would have been saved many days or weeks of pain and misery if they had died on the beach.

As it turned out, in the next three months almost all of us who started into action on L-day were casualties, as were many of the replacements who came in later. If the beach had been defended, it all would probably have been over with quickly.

Also, if there had been a fight on the beach, Ernie Pyle would have had a chance to learn about our war, the war in the Pacific. He could have written the truth about it, then.

We knew about Ernie Pyle, the kind of a man he was and what he wrote about. In her letters my mother praised him for his honesty and for the sacrifices he made in bringing the line company's story to the home front. For many months we had all hoped that he could finally come to our side of the world, to see and tell about *our* war. But when he came, he first stopped at the beautiful rear-island supply bases, and he got a very erroneous impression. When he finally joined marines headed into the war, his initial encounter was the first few days on Okinawa, days that were unusually quiet from the standpoint of combat. Before he had been in the area long enough to get a taste of what our war was really like, he was dead. His accounts of his few days there are misleading and create a misconception for posterity.

For months, Ernie lived in and wrote about the tough war in Europe, but in the easy little war we were fighting with the Japs, he was killed in a couple of weeks. That kind of tells you something, doesn't it?

I am sure he had no idea of what he would have seen had he lived through the easy part of our war. I have read, in one of his articles from the Pacific, that the "old infantry soldier [in Europe] was still the bottom of the ditch." I would like to see what he would have written if he could have been with us at Wana Draw or Awacha Pocket or the Shuri line. Marines were assault troops, it's true, but once ashore they were just light infantry with their own philosophy of how to win. I believe Ernie would have found that, for front-line troops facing a formidable enemy, war was a miserable common experience.

It was also unfortunate that, even had he lived, Ernie had gotten there too late to experience the special effects of fighting in the jungle. He was such a talented writer that I would certainly like to read his description of it. I have never read anything approaching an adequate description of jungle warfare. An enormous expenditure of energy is required under very trying natural conditions. The heat feels almost like an extra, heavy weight upon you. Insects and reptiles are constant concerns, and there is an eeriness about fighting in the jungle. You can't see very far even in the daytime. Snipers in daylight and infiltrators after dark have you at a great disadvantage. There is a peculiar apprehension in the jungle that you never forget. Anyway, Ernie missed all that. He never got to tell the world about the tougher part of our island war because he was killed too soon in the easier part.

For several days some of us had it so easy that it actually scared us. We knew that it could never last.

We had landed between Yontan and Kadena airfields. The Sixth Marine Division landed on our left and army divisions of the Twenty-fourth Corps on our right. When we were all inland for some distance, the Sixth Marine Division turned north and the army divisions turned south. The First Marine Division went straight on across the island. The Sixth and the army both ran into heavy fighting, but we moved with unbelievable ease. When we had crossed the island, we set up beach defenses to deter the Japs from making counterlandings behind the other units.

In the last letter home before we assaulted Okinawa, expecting to die, I had tried to tell the folks how I felt about them. I did such a poor job of it that I am embarrassed to quote that part of the letter. Mom's note on the back says "Written Mch 23 — Recd Apr. 1 — 9 days en route, Easter Sunday." The date they received it, April Fool's Day, was the day we landed on Okinawa — April 1, 1945.

> Dearest Mom and Dad,
>   This will probably reach you after quite an absence of letters from me. I am sorry. All is well.
>   You mentioned my not dating my letters. I just figured it wasn't worth the bothering with.
>   Today is the twenty-third day of March in the hectic year of 1945. . . .
>   I do remember Johnny McCree well, Mom. I believe I have done my Irish justice so far. Everything is dandy so don't worry and we'll see.
>   All my love and heart to you now and forever.
>   Jim

In one of her letters to me, Mother had asked if I remembered Johnny McCree. From the days when I was very young, in times of stress or trouble, Mother had sung a little song that ended "It'll all come right / by tomorrow night, / says Johnny McCree today." I wondered what Johnny would have said if he were going in on Okinawa in a few days, but thoughts of the old song were comforting, anyway.

After we crossed the island, we eventually set up and dug in on some high ground for nighttime positions and sent out patrols each morning.

For several days, about all the action we had with the enemy was occasional contact with individuals or small groups on our daylight patrols, or infiltrators and scouts feeling out our positions at night. That isn't to say there weren't some very precarious and worrisome times.

Wyman Basinger, a close friend of mine from Jefferson City, Missouri, was leader of the third section of machine guns in E Company. While on one of the patrols, Basinger and his men encountered a group of Japs that had laid an ambush for them. Eckhard Muessig, one of Basinger's squad leaders, who was from Ohio, discovered the Japs before they could spring their attack, and he damn near wiped them out by himself.

The Jap bombers that flew over every night came close to us on several occasions, but it was by accident. Their primary targets were far enough away that we were comparatively safe from that quarter.

We had some new experiences with night activity because of the civilian population. Prior to Okinawa we had killed whatever moved in on us at night. During the first few days on Okinawa, some of our men had the distasteful and unfortunate experience of killing women and children. They were afraid to come out of their hiding places during the day, when we could easily have identified them as civilians. Instead they chose to come out at night, thinking it was safer. To see in the morning the bodies of the civilians they had killed in the night, especially the children, was abhorrent to the marines. So they began to let people get close enough to them in the night to be identified as soldiers or civilians.

That proved to be a mistake, however. Soon the Jap soldiers were wearing clothing that would silhouette them as women and get them through our lines. When they were behind our lines, they tossed grenades into the positions they had passed. The marines resumed killing whatever approached them at night.

We tried to inform the civilians in every way possible that they should not make any movement at night, including loudspeaker announcements and pamphlets. We did everything we could to make sure of our targets, but it was almost impossible in the dark. We could not wait until they tried to kill us before committing ourselves, and many more civilians died, either because they didn't get the word or because they chose to ignore it. It was one of the many lamentable fortunes of war.

When Lieutenant Calley was brought to task for killing civilians in Vietnam, it brought back memories of some of the killing we did on that part of Okinawa. Even though I wasn't in sympathy with what Calley did, I couldn't agree with our government's treatment of him. I believe that when you send young men into such places, you abandon any right to question whatever they do.

One quiet night, from one of my gun positions I heard Joe Lunsford's voice ring out, "Halt!" There was a flurry of sound and movement, followed by the rumbling bark of a burst of light machine-gun fire. Then all was quiet. The entire line of defense was instantly wide awake and remained that way for the rest of the night. I crawled over to the gun position and stayed there until dawn. In the first light of morning, we could see that Joe had riddled one of the Okinawan's horses. We passed the word. Everyone breathed a sigh of relief and, after posting guard watches, took turns getting what rest they could before the day's activity began.

When the sun was well up in the sky and everyone was awake, one of the rifle squad leaders began to tease Joe for cutting loose with the gun, scaring the shit out of everyone. Whenever the guns opened up, it generally meant an attack on us. I knew the squad leader well. He was a good man and a good marine. He had been a BAR man close to our position that first bloody night on Peleliu.

I spoke to Joe, but I was smiling at the squad leader when I said, "Hey, how about that, Joe? Maybe next time we better let whatever it is go right on through."

That changed the complexion of things. We all had a good laugh over losing a little sleep but having no casualties. I guess, in our hearts, we were all saying our thanks for having buddies like Joe to look out for our asses while we slept.

All of us who knew what war really was were deeply grateful for those precious comparatively peaceful days, and we did everything we could to keep them that way. In that nice, quiet atmosphere some of the new guys, without realizing what fools they were making of themselves, got a little enthusiastic about souvenirs.

One of the replacements that joined us shortly before the Okinawan campaign was a fellow named Anderson, a tough young guy by civilian standards, who had been fairly successful at some amateur boxing. He was quite cocky, not really arrogant, but pretty chesty. I know he figured the Marine Corps was the place for him. Poor Anderson. At first he was a little reserved, in respect for the men with experience in combat. After a few days of the surprisingly easy time of it we had at the start of Okinawa, he decided combat wasn't so tough. He got ill-advisedly confident and, unbeknown to me, he started reconnoitering the caves around us. When I found out about it, I lit into him, "Anderson, you stupid fucker! If I want you to go into some cave, I'll tell you. Up until I do tell you, stay the hell out of the caves. Do you hear me?"

I embarrassed him and pissed him off at the same time. He challenged me, "If you think you're so tough, Johnston, I'll fight you here and now."

"Listen, boy," I answered, "You don't understand the corps at all. I don't have to whip you to tell you what you're going to do. I'm your section leader. That's all that's required. I'll tell you something else — you're a tough guy now but we'll see how tough you are when the shit starts flying. Before we're through with this island, you'll be so fuckin' much smarter than you are now that you can't imagine it. When this is over, if you still feel like fighting and we're still alive, I'll be glad to knock the shit out of you just on general principles. Up until then, you better learn damn quick to do what I tell you, or you'll damn sure live to regret it."

He was a good kid. He just didn't realize I was trying to give him a better chance of living long enough to find out what he'd gotten himself into. I had told all the boys to stay out of the caves. I knew that if I didn't give them hell about it, some of the new men who had never been in battle would probably be sneaking into the caves looking for souvenirs. At least they would do that until someone ran into a cave that was trapped or ambushed and we had to carry out bodies or patched-up stumps of arms or legs. I knew if I could keep them alive until they had been in a few firefights, or mortar and artillery barrages, the chances would be a lot better that they wouldn't get themselves killed or maimed by foolishly poking around someplace.

God have mercy! Battle is so intimidating, so humbling. It was pitiful to watch the new men come in, carefree and unbothered, insouciant and confident, and then see what was left when battle had wiped all that innocence away. I almost wished that Anderson could stay cocky, though he would then probably have given me a beating. He outweighed me by many pounds. I was quite certain, however, that his brashness wouldn't last, whether I liked it or not.

I once read about a Union Civil War commander who boasted that his outfit, on the move, could butcher a hog and never stop their march. I'm sure they were a good outfit, but they didn't have anything on us. On one of our early Okinawan patrols, my buddy Joe butchered a pig by himself, and we never stopped. We never even slowed down.

As we patrolled we saw a small pig running across a field. Joe said, "Jim, we should get that pig."

I answered, "Yeah, Joe, but I don't know what to do with it. I've never killed anything but men."

Joe replied, "I know how. If you'll carry my gear I'll kill him, butcher him, and catch you as soon as I can."

"Done," I said.

We stepped off to the side of the line of march. Joe dumped his gear and with one well-placed shot killed the pig at about a hundred yards. He ran down and bled the pig and started to butcher. I picked up his gear and ran back to lead my men. In a half hour or so, Joe caught up with us. He had a tree limb across his shoulders, with part of the butchered pig on each end of the limb. We split up the loads — his gear, my gear, and the pork — for the rest of the patrol. When we went back to our temporary area, we cooked the pig in a big, black Okinawan pot we had scrounged. After we had eaten our fill, we passed the rest of the meat out to our troops, for as long as it lasted.

For the corps in wartime, conditions at that point on Okinawa were too good to be true, though we did suffer a couple of unexpected unpleasantries.

The little mosquitoes on Okinawa were about half the size of the big jungle babies we were used to, but they were every bit as powerful and stung immediately upon contact. Something new, the fleas, chewed on us incessantly. Fleas may not seem significant in a war zone, but these little bastards were wicked. They were thick on us, and they gave us real nasty bites all night long. Until those in charge arranged to bring us a powder that controlled them, the fleas didn't allow anyone a peaceful rest for any decent length of time. The powder was very effective. It was fun to douse ourselves and our gear and watch the little bastards come out of the seams. After that we could get some sleep. There was plenty of water to drink, and for a little while there were even some vegetables from the Okinawans' gardens. We had some fresh cabbage stews and the like. Life was wonderful and we prayed it could last. Could it be that the Japs would give up?

The next letter home is postmarked April 11, 1945.

Dearest Mom and Dad,

Everything is going fine — all is well.

I was reading a book of Hemingway's works a while back in which he quoted Shakespeare. "By my troth I care not: a man can die but once; we owe God a death . . . and let it go which way it will, he that dies this year is quit for the next."

I got some letters from you, two from [a girl], and one from a Marine buddy yesterday.

I guess Mike is back to duty from his furlough by now.[1] I wonder if he got married. I rather doubt it.

It has been quite a long time since I've written but hope you haven't worried too much. I'm sorry I couldn't do anything about the anniversaries you mentioned. I hope we can celebrate the next ones together.

Jim

The next letter is postmarked April 18, 1945.

Dearest Mom and Dad,

Am receiving your mail in good order. It is great — as always. Am rushed for time and don't have much paper but this will let you know that all is well so far. I'm on Okinawa in the Ryukyu Islands so you guessed right. It isn't far to Japan from here. It has been easy going so far — big surprise to me. Guess we surprised them hitting this close to home. Lots of bombing. May get rough a little later. Don't know where or what from here. Hope and pray!!! home — maybe. Joe is well and going strong — good boy!

God bless you my people. Gotta quit for now.

Jim

As I wrote those letters, I was pipe-dreaming: Maybe we had neutralized much of the Jap strength. Maybe, for once, we had overestimated their strength. Maybe the army and the Sixth Marine Division could handle their objectives. Maybe we would be fortunate enough to draw a soft spot, like the Second Marine Division that was still offshore in reserve. If it all smoothed out that way, by the time we could mount another campaign I would have so much time overseas that I might get a leave for a few days. I could see home and the folks. I'd been gone from home and the girls I knew for about two and a half years. Young female companionship (strange as it may seem, even a girl just to talk to) occupied a lot of my thoughts. I was satisfied that if I could only spend a couple of weeks in the peaceful, civilian environment of home, I would be ready to get back to the Pacific Theater with a fresh attitude. Maybe I could even make some China duty and have some tall tales to tell the boots when it was over.

Then I would awaken in the night to the rumbling of the artillery down south, and I would say to myself, "Jimmy, don't be a dumb-ass thinking about going home. When you started in here, you knew you would probably die here. Things haven't changed. They have just moved around a little. This is Okinawa. You're a marine. Don't let this little soft spell fool you. Pretty soon the shit will hit the fan. If it doesn't, you'll have to make Japan before you have a chance to see home."

My next letter to the folks is written on Jap paper. It is dated April 19, 1945. I was writing every chance I had.

Dearest Mom and Dad,

Just received the letter telling of the farm sale.[2] Yes, that is fine with me. I'm a westerner at heart. One thing I want you to know is this — you said I might be embarrassed of the farm or ashamed of it. I will not be ashamed of anything there or any-where. People's opinions have come to mean very little to me and besides it would have to be far worse than I know it could be there before it would be near as bad as I have seen the best of people in over here. So conditions are conditions and so is cir-cumstance, circumstance, and chance is what makes one person something while another isn't quite so much. So pomp and splendor and luxuries and fine things are not too dear to me. I have seen proud and vain men crawl on their bellies through the mud and I've seen brave men with the light of terrible fear in their eyes — so what people are and think is little. They are only the way they are at times and would be different in a different place. I believe I have seen humanity at its worst in about every way and I hope I have learned to be neither vain nor ashamed but to try to be happy and appreciative for what God has cast to be my lot. I would not have been ashamed but I like the west so am happy that things are as they are. I have no idea what will happen here now or soon. I doubt now, since so far this one has not been too blood and guts, that I will get home soon. Probably another one if I last this one out. Lots of Marines have stayed two years and a half. It is rather disheartening because, perhaps foolishly, I had rather expected to go home after this one. I guess

that is the best way to look at it. Seriously — we never know
what is coming or what is best, so, "Never complain or explain,"
eh, Pop? Someone must fight the war and I'm doing a pretty
good job so far. Must close for this time — God bless you and
my heart to you always.

Jim

All the letters I wrote during that period reflect two things: wishful
thinking that our allied divisions could finish their assignments without
help from us, and realistic expectancy that we would soon be called into
the middle of the heavy fighting. Each day we hoped the boys down
south could finish it up, each night the barrages of artillery, naval gunfire, and bombing continued.

One day late in April, the uncertainty ended when we got the word
that we were moving south. Trucks came to transport us, which was a
new experience. This wasn't good. They needed us too badly to wait for
us to walk. The trucks unloaded us behind the front and we moved into
the lines, to relieve an army division during a heavy enemy mortar and
artillery barrage. As we moved up I passed one young soldier-boy sitting
beside the little trail road. His hand was badly bleeding from a shrapnel
wound. He just sat there looking at it. I said to him, "Lad, you'd better
get that patched up."

He answered, "I don't know how."

"Where's your corpsman — your medic?"

"I don't know."

I hollered "Corpsman!" and Doc Lindeman came running.

Allan Lindeman was a tall, slim boy, one of the navy pharmacist's
mates who went with us and patched us up when we were wounded. All
the corpsmen that I knew in the war were a credit to the Marine Corps,
every one. Allan Lindeman was among the best of the best. He was
killed on Okinawa.

He bandaged the kid's hand with a compress and started him back
down the road, over the hill to a rear area. We went forward to our destination — the front lines. When we got there the area stunk terribly.

The bodies of young American soldiers lay decomposing on top of the ground.

We clipped the bottom dog tags off the soldiers' bodies (the ones that had tags) and sent them to graves registration as best we could. We buried the decomposing remains, where at least the fucking flies couldn't work on them.

We were on the front face of a sizable hill, completely exposed to a concealed, well-fortified, well-equipped enemy. The Japs had made up their minds that no matter how futile their efforts to stop us, they would make as many of us die as they could. The Japs had bountiful ordnance and used it against us. Several times there were up to sixty rounds per hour of high explosives landing in our company area, both day and night. In addition to the artillery, they had several 90mm mortar batteries as well as many smaller mortars, like the ones we called knee mortars. (That big stuff could really wreck things. One day while there I happened to be looking at Jess Bowman, a Third Platoon rifleman from Tennessee, when one of the artillery rounds went off damn near under him. It blew him what I would guess to be about twenty feet in the air and he came down like a rag doll. I figured he was dead for certain, but I found out after the war that he had somehow lived to tell about it.) They also had a most effectively disguised and fortified line of interlocking, mutually supporting small arms positions.

When the troop movements stopped, us moving in and the army division moving out, the enemy artillery and mortars abated noticeably. Lamm, one of my squad leaders, started to reconnoiter the area to define our situation. When you set up a machine gun, you needed to know what you were doing; otherwise you could kill a bunch of your own men in a hurry. It wasn't possible to determine the direction of the departing army division's front or the position of remaining friendly forces.

The soldiers of the army division that we were relieving were deployed in such a helter-skelter fashion that we could discern very little about which way they were trying to go or what was happening. I asked one of them if they had an officer. He pointed at one of the rotting bodies and told me that was their lieutenant. I asked who was in charge, but no one answered. I asked if there was a corporal there. One young fellow responded that he was a corporal. I asked him, "What's the word?"

Had I asked most marine corporals that question, they would have told me the status quo — past, present, and expected. The army corporal didn't know what I meant. He was a good boy, as I know they all were, and he wanted to help. But, like his fellow soldiers in that division, he hadn't been given the consideration and respect he deserved. He hadn't gotten the teaching he so badly needed in the place he found himself.

The Jap artillery was fierce. I asked the corporal if it was always like that, and he said that it had been bad for some time. I asked if there wasn't something we could do about it, and he said he sure as hell didn't know what. I asked if they had tried to advance out of their area and he said, "Not lately."

One of the army machine gunners there was firing burst after burst through a 1917A1 at nothing. He made a good sighting point for the Jap artillery. I told him I thought it would be a good idea to quit firing, and he did. Before long the artillery and mortar fire eased off to sporadic firing. Word came for the army unit to move back and they were soon gone.

We hadn't the slightest idea of what was going on, except that we were getting the shit pounded out of us. Lamm was extending his area of search, trying to establish some kind of order out of the hodge-podge that the army division had left us, when a Jap automatic weapon opened up on him. One slug tore up his leg very badly. I had to cut away his trousers so that the corpsman could work on him. I kidded him about a twenty-five-dollar wound — a ticket home — but his color was bad. I wasn't surprised when I heard he had died on the way to the hospital, but I was deeply saddened. He had been such a good and trusted friend for a long time.

Joe Lunsford took over leadership of Lamm's squad. Very ably, I might add. I went with Joe and Wiley Brown, my other squad leader, to pick out spots for their men and guns, and then looked for a spot for myself. I finally wound up in a little pig sty along with a young company runner, Bako. We cleaned up the place as best we could. It was about six or seven feet long and maybe five feet wide. The walls were different heights, running from about two feet or so in front to three feet, or a little higher, in back. The sty had a half roof of sticks and straw that got ripped to ribbons by artillery and mortar shrapnel in the days that we were there. The sty was easy to see. It wasn't camouflaged in any way. I am sure the Japs tried to hit it directly, for shell holes were close to it on every side. The walls were pocked by shrapnel hits all around, but to our great good fortune the Japs never got it centered.

There was a gently sloping valley in front of us, running parallel to our lines. The ground sloped down from our positions about forty or fifty yards to the valley's bottom and then up for another forty or fifty yards to a ridge on the other side. In the low part of the little valley was a disabled and abandoned army tank. The valley extended to our right, what I would estimate as five hundred yards, the ground then rising rather quickly to a prominent rocky hill. On the other side of the ridge in front of us, unknown to us at that time, was a great, deep gorge known as Awacha Pocket. From there a valley ran all the way west to the sea.

From our position we began a series of attacks, testing different tactics that might neutralize the Jap defenses in front of us.

We came into that area not knowing what was going on there, and we spent the lives of a lot of good men finding out. Behind the high rocky hill on our right the Japs had antitank artillery. Their projectiles were not very large — probably 47MM or the like — but very fast, and their effectiveness was evidenced by the dead army tank in the little valley in front of us. The turret cover on it was open and a Jap sniper had gotten into it. We tried to get him with rifle fire, to no avail. A marine named Gines then got a grenade launcher for his rifle and from quite a distance, miraculously, dropped a grenade into that little opening in the top of the tank.

Our time at Awacha Pocket was a study in futility and frustration for me. Much of Okinawa was that way, with three or four places that were possible exceptions. We were facing a formidable foe. Either we manned the most forward defensive positions, or we were so close to the riflemen in assaults that we could bring our firepower to bear in a matter of seconds. We were always in the enemy's direct line of sight. We took a hell of a beating from small arms fire, mortars and artillery and we never did get in a position to enjoy the grim satisfaction of slaughtering the Japs. Not like we had that first night on Peleliu.

Machine guns work best against masses charging at you. To shoot at areas, or isolated individuals, is not often practical. Pattern firing is highly inefficient. Good rifle fire is most effective against individuals. The machine-gun position is static, and when you open up the guns, the position is positively identified for enemy mortar, artillery, and sniper fire. It is ridiculous to get your gunners killed off that way unless you have enemy concentrations worth the cost, concentrations against which the guns are the most effective response.

Except for the insurance against counterattacks that the machine guns provided, we would have been better off on Okinawa to have had BARS or MIS[3] and our own personal ammo. Instead, we carried the heavy machine-gun shit all over the island and never did get a chance to use the guns effectively.

One day at Awacha, Utter told me our CO had asked him about the possibility of me taking charge of "a bunch" of riflemen. Our ranks were so depleted that it was impossible to tell what had been squads or platoons. When something needed to be done, we took "a bunch" of what was left and went after it. Utter said he had talked the CO out of it, saying I was the best machine-gun man in the battalion. Utter was trying to protect me from taking on new, unfamiliar duties in the midst of battle. I was, of course, grateful for his concern, but I was sorely disappointed that I didn't have the choice of taking the job. I was sick of taking the beating "lying down." I'd have been pleased to have a job where I had a chance to be more effective against the enemy.

I was tired and frustrated from taking the constant pounding, with no chance to see something against which we could put the guns to work. But I knew better than to get impatient and fire our guns at nothing but air. That would just be a simple-minded way to get a lot of marines killed.

Wiley Brown must have felt much the same way. We had started one assault, stalled in wide-open terrain, and were taking all kinds of fire when Wiley finally stood straight up and said loudly, "By God, let's do something even if it's wrong." Old buddy Brown had made up his mind that, though it might or might not be right to charge into the Japs' trenches, it would beat the hell out of sitting there in one place doing nothing, taking a beating like a puppy dog. What we were getting done by doing nothing was damn sure wrong.

It hadn't been many days after my discussion about caves with Anderson that we were sitting around in a shelled-out area awaiting word to move when one of my boys came to me. He had someone with him, a young, obviously inexperienced stranger wearing clean dungarees and carrying a brand-new tommy gun. This boot was from some rear-echelon supply outfit, and some chickenshit noncom had been chewing him a new asshole. The boot had an idea that the corps would be a different situation, so he took off from his own unit to get into the war, away from the bastard that was making him miserable. Noble but foolish. As unreasonable as it was for him to put up with the crap he was taking from some horseshit asshole, it still beat the hell out of war, and I told him so. "Go back to your outfit, swallow your tongue and your pride, and thank God someone is not blowing your ass away. Look at Anderson, there. He thought he was a tough son of a bitch till we got in the war. Now his tail is so far between his legs he could chew on the end of it."

Anderson looked over at me but never said a word, not one fucking word. Having been indoctrinated by means of a few days of death and destruction, Anderson had become a pussycat, just like all the rest of us.

I put my arm on the young boot's shoulder and said, "Lad, this is no game. If you stay here, by the time you find out what a mistake you've made, it will be too late. I don't want to be responsible for letting you make that much of a chump of yourself. Go back over the hill where you came from. Get back where you're supposed to be, and pray you can live long enough to get home."

He turned his back to me and walked off out of sight. That was the last I ever saw or heard of him.

I don't know for sure whatever became of Anderson. He got sick and left for the company sick bay before we had been down south very long.

I don't know whether he ever came back and, if he did come back, whether he lived or died. However it went, I am not running him down. Like all the other inexperienced people, he just didn't know what the war was like. Maybe he talked a little too much before he found out, but he certainly wasn't alone in that regard.

We had been at Awacha a few days when I got a long letter from my grandfather. He was a Scotsman of the old ilk, courageous and dedicated.

Gramps was my pal. Once in a while he would slip me a quarter. That was in the "dirty thirties," when money was really tight, and I don't know where in the world he got the coin. With that quarter, I could see a movie, buy a big box of buttered popcorn and a bottle of grape pop. One time when I was young, I got the flu real bad and just about died. When I woke up in the night, Gramps was sitting there in a chair by my bed. Grandpa had always done everything he could to make my life better. He was a rock to me.

In his letter he wrote of several different happenings and several people, and at the end he wrote that he was proud of me and my fellow marines. It gave me a real boost. Now, each time I go to the little country cemetery here in Nebraska, and read the date on my grandfather's tombstone, I feel emotions I cannot explain. The date is April 13, 1945. Gramps had already died when I got his letter and, it seemed, was even trying to help me from beyond the veil.

How I wish I still had his letter, but it was nearly impossible to save something like that in the field. If we tried to keep anything made of paper, it would soon get wet and so torn that it was not readable. Also, we almost always had to crumple up paper, slick or otherwise, and use it to wipe our asses.

On one occasion we began an attack all along that part of our lines. We pushed out as far as we could but again came under intense fire, both artillery and small arms, and were suffering quite heavy casualties. We took what cover we could find. Walt Knowles, Brown, and I found a shell hole and crawled into it. Brown and Knowles laid on their backs against the front of the hole. They were a few feet in front of and facing me. I was looking forward, past them, to see what was ahead for us. As I watched, the Japs behind a ridge a few yards in front of us began to send a mortar barrage at us. The Japs were so close that the propelling charges on their mortars were very light, and I could see the shells floating lazily at us. The sky seemed to be filled with them.

When I first saw the shells in the sky, I told Brown and Knowles about them. I had played a lot of ball in school, both baseball and softball, and was a pretty good judge of where a fly ball would come down. As I watched the mortar shells in the sky, getting thicker and thicker, I noticed one shell on its ascent headed straight at the hole we were in. I was kneeling in the hole and I started to stand up to run.

I told the two, "Oh shit, boys, here comes one that's going to light in this hole."

As we all started to move out, it began to look like the shell would land behind us. I said, "No, it ain't gonna light here," and we all hit the deck again.

When the damn thing started down, again it appeared to be headed right into the hole with us. I said, "Yeah, it is," and we all started out of the hole again.

Just a split second before it lit, I judged it would be short. Again, "No, it ain't."

I pushed Brown and Knowles flat and hit the deck with them. That shell lit where we could reach out and touch the hole it made in the ground. If the ground had been hard the concussion of the exploding shell would probably have killed the three of us. As it was, the round sunk so far in the soft earth that the explosion was significantly muffled. It blew mud all over us, but that was it.

The rest of my men were all behind us, where they could watch the show I put on for them. As long thereafter as we were together, they would occasionally kid me about it. They would mimic my actions up and down, repeating, "Yeah, it is . . . no it ain't." It was good for many a laugh, even though it concerned a time when split-second judgment had meant the difference between life and death for Brown and Knowles and me. Of course, in that terrible place there were many times when snap decisions were all you had time for, and death waited patiently for you to make the wrong choice.

We were in the Awacha Pocket area for around a couple of weeks. I always wondered if we couldn't have found positions that wouldn't have been quite so vulnerable. We stopped exactly where the Japs wanted us — in wide-open country, completely visible, and exposed to every kind of fire they had.

Frenchie was killed there, by mortars. Like Lamm, Kollman and Marion Black and a little marine named Kelly were killed by small arms fire.

As I said, we attacked several times and in different ways, trying to gain ground and destroy the enemy. First we tried the old Marine Corps standby — the direct frontal assault. That didn't work, but we did find out that there were machine guns in place with the antitank artillery. Next time we laid down a mortar and artillery barrage about 150 yards to our front, then some smoke. We got out to the rim of the big valley. We sent one of our sister-platoons on our left flank around the bend of the valley for a way, but they soon came under fire from the caves on the north wall of the big draw and took heavy casualties. After trying a number of approaches, we finally found a plan that worked.

We sent tanks and infantry around the left flank, where the infantry had tried to go alone. The combination got to a position where they could bring fire to bear on the Japs in the valley caves, the ones that had stopped the advances on our flanks. Thus the linemen and tanks on the right could get over the brink of the hill and knock out the gun positions behind it. Simultaneously, we in E Company moved through the draw in front of us.

In one book I have read, the author alludes to the work of the Fifth Marines at that time as not being so desultory that a good man couldn't be wounded (the good man being a future U.S. senator, Major Paul Douglas, who was shot in the arm). I doubt that my buddies who died in that place would agree with the author's assessment of the situation as being anywhere near "desultory." For damn sure I don't. And I didn't get my ideas about it from a book I read or from what someone told me. I was there.

Shortly before we left the area of Awacha Pocket, I had an experience that profoundly affected me, in a way that has endured over the years. I alluded to it earlier in recounting my experience with the little white cloud on Peleliu.

One night, while I lay in the Okinawan pig sty during a prolonged Jap artillery barrage, I was stricken with a series of convulsions. It was beyond my power to control them. First I tried to tighten every muscle in my body. Then I tried to relax every muscle. I tried to control my reflexes with my mind but to no avail. I prayed that the artillery rounds, as they came in, would either light far away in an open field, where they would hurt no one, or that they would light in the sty with me and make a quick job of it. I did my best to keep little Bako, the replacement who was in the sty with me, from sensing my spasms. Everything I tried was futile. I finally just gave up and let the convulsions run their course. After a while they subsided. Later they ceased entirely and I fell into a deep sleep. I didn't tell the corpsman, or anyone, about the convulsions. I would have died there rather than leave because of the convulsions.

Battle is extremely demanding, menial, arduous endeavor. It is unbelievably depleting both physically and mentally, and the nature of our circumstances was starting to take its toll on me. In addition to the exertion required to fight, I worried a great deal about my responsibility to my men.

In battle, you seldom have a chance to rest until you are near a state of total exhaustion. Even when you sleep under those conditions, your instincts are so finely honed in the interest of survival that the tiniest sound, such as a twig snapping, will sometimes shock you instantly wide awake. Strangely enough, on the other hand, you can sometimes sleep soundly through a mortar barrage. It is often difficult to discern between the conscious and the subconscious — dreams or reality, being asleep or being awake.

Sometime during that night I became aware of something close above me. When I looked up, I saw the countenance of a beautiful Lady. Beneath her smiling face there were wisps of veil-like garments but no recognizable form. She spoke quietly but clearly, saying, "Don't be afraid. You will go home in a strange way." I was instantly wide awake. I searched the darkness of the Okinawan night for some lingering evidence of what I had seen. Silently, I earnestly beseeched the Lady to return and explain her meaning. I lay awake for some time, then eventually went to sleep. In the morning, when I awakened, I could not have been positive whether I had seen the Lady while I was asleep or awake. There was one thing for certain, though. There was a great transformation in me. I was no longer afraid. In the days that followed, when I thought of the Lady and wondered about it all, I sometimes thought of the old verse: "Goodbye cruel world, / I'm going home. / Thou art not my friend / and I'm not thine." Perhaps that was the "home" to which I would go "in a strange way." But I was at peace with myself. I had made up my mind that I wouldn't give up. I would do the very best I could, but whether I lived or died, it was OK by me. I still clung to life, but the words kept coming back to me, "By my troth I care not. / A man can die but once."

I consciously began a different personal behavior pattern after that. I always kept the lives of my men uppermost in my mind and tried watchfully to care for them. However, I looked especially for tasks that I could do alone, or with just a few of the men, work that would give me the satisfaction of doing something. Something, like Brown had said, even if it was wrong.

In the years since Okinawa, thousands of times I have thought of the Lady who came to me that night in the little pig sty. In my darkest hours, the memory of Her has brought me peace, and I have often wondered if I shall ever see Her again.

When we left Awacha Pocket, we fought night and day from one ridge to the next hill — Wilson Ridge, Wana Ridge, Hill 55, Wana Draw — fighting nearly as hard to get down the forward sides of promentories as we had fought to get up them in the first place.

In the proximity of that time and place, we had two new experiences with Jap weapons. First, the Japs started sending over a huge explosive missile that we called buzz bombs because of the sound they made in flight. I've heard them called other things, such as mallet mortars, because of the way their propelling charge was fired. In flight they sounded *buzz — buzz — buzz.* When that sound quit, you wanted to be out of their line of flight, if possible, because that was when they started down. They carried a very large explosive charge and made a hell of a noise when they went off. Fortunately, none of them ever came down in our midst.

The second new sound came when the Japs turned twin 20MM automatic anti-aircraft guns down on us as antipersonnel weapons. The twenties had explosive projectiles like artillery. When they were directed at us, the firing of the gun, the sound of the shell in flight, and the explosion of the shell when it hit made a very weird, disturbing sound. They were very lethal.

One time in that tangle of days, I was on a little hill where we had captured one of the twin 20MM positions. I was looking at the Jap guns when I noticed some of our riflemen start across a small depression fifty yards to my left. As the marines moved against a hill on the other side of the valley, a Jap threw a grenade into their midst. One of the marines smothered it with his body, killing himself but saving some of his friends.

He was a tall, slim, stoop-shouldered southerner (from one of the Carolinas I think, though I didn't know him well). To my knowledge, several Medals of Honor have been given posthumously for exactly the same well-defined, selfless, and brave act of sacrifice.

Knowing that, I tried to get someone to acknowledge the man's deed that I had witnessed, but to no avail. Everyone was too occupied, or indifferent to the man personally, or unapproving of something he had done that didn't fit the corps's mold. It was but another incident that strengthened my feelings about medals for valor. Courage is in a man's own heart. No one but God can measure the courage in a man's heart or compare it with the courage in other men's hearts.

We eventually made our way to a ridge about five hundred yards from the town of Shuri, approximately half a mile inland from Naha.

From that ridge we could see at our front the remains of the concrete barracks in the town. At the time we thought those were the remnants of Shuri Castle, a renowned structure that had been visited by Admiral Perry in the nineteenth century. There had been another unit of marines on the ridge before we got there. That is the only place I ever saw where marines had dug trenches between their foxholes. Once again we were on the receiving end of intense concentrations of artillery, mortar, and small arms fire. Little Gines of the rifle grenade, and my friend Jack Davis from Lyman, Nebraska, were wounded there. A man named Gosman in one of my gun crews was killed. The bullet that killed him first passed closely in front of my face. When the bullet hit Gosman's head, it sounded as if someone had hit a ripe watermelon with a baseball bat. He fell where I could reach him by extending my arm, but he might as well have fallen alone in the desert, for he was dead when he hit the ground.

We moved a little way to tie in with an outfit on our right. We established our position and toward evening Utter came up and told me to expect a tank attack after dark. Reports had come in of someone hearing tank motors directly to our front. I asked, "What should I do, Leon, throw rocks at them? Can you get a bazooka?"

Utter said he would arrange for a battery of artillery to zero in a few yards in front of us, so if the tanks did attack us we could call for the artillery support in the night. Minutes after Utter left us, a few rounds of our artillery hit sixty or seventy yards in front of us, to designate and verify the area. I felt a lot better. We knew how to place grenades on the tank tracks to disable them but that wasn't a pleasant experience to anticipate.

We stayed on the ridge for a couple of days, attempting two assaults across the valley that was between us and Shuri.

Earlier in the campaign, following one of our unsuccessful assaults on Awacha Pocket, we had been given the word to return to our original positions. I had led my section out by habit, because I always went in front of my men. Brown, on the other hand, had waited 'til last and had followed his men out. That is what I should have done. Brown wasn't any braver than I was, but in some ways he was smarter.

I was happy when I got another chance to handle a withdrawal. My chance came in our first attempt to move across the valley in front of Shuri. In the vernacular of World War I, we went "over the top," out of our trenches into the attack on the Jap stronghold. We met formidable, efficient resistance. Again, as at Awacha, we took too many casualties, and it was obvious that our approach wasn't practical. When the word came to return to our original position, I told Brown to take the section back. I waited 'til everyone else was out and I came back last. It was very gratifying. I think even Brown appreciated it. I know he was glad to get moving quickly, for we were catching a barrage of pretty good-sized mortars. Blood was running out the ears of one of his men as they moved back.

Something happened in front of Shuri that was funny, in a morbid sort of way. Old bitcher Brown came over where Joe and I were holed up and started his chant about how we should change positions with his squad because they had been catching a lot of fire for quite a while. I pointed at the track of an artillery shell that had caught the edge of our foxhole that morning and said, "Are they coming any closer than that, Wiley?"

The place I pointed to was an indentation where a Jap artillery shell had hit the sloping rear edge of our foxhole. If it had hit half an inch lower, its point would have struck the dirt and sent Joe and me to kingdom come. As it happened, the curved surface of the shell made contact with the edge in such a way that it skipped off the ground, much like the flat rocks you throw to skip on water. The shell ricocheted back up into the air, hit a little tree fifteen or twenty yards behind us, and blew away the whole top of the tree.

Brown said, "Shit, Johnston, that didn't happen just now."

I said, "Yeah it did, Wiley. If you'd like to see for yourself, stick around a little while. If things keep up like they have been, it won't be long 'til it happens again." Brown hustled back where he'd come from.

As we began to move down into the valley on our second assault, the rifle squad leader immediately behind me was hit in the leg by automatic small arms fire. The bullets popped the air loudly close by my head. Later, I noticed two bullet holes in the left side of the flap on my back pack, and it was easy for me to hypothesize that the bullets that hit the rifleman's leg had first gone through my pack.

We attacked across the valley, taking casualties as expected. A Mexican-American lad who was one of our gunners was killed. His wife had written that she was sleeping with one of his friends and that, after all, he'd been gone three months and he surely couldn't expect her to wait forever. That had made me feel angry at her and bad for him, even before he died.

As we moved forward we came to a ridge that stretched across our front. We paused there. Some of the marines in the unit on our right flank (I believe it was the Fourth Marines) hollered to us that there was a cave on the back side of the knoll we were on, and that they were exposed to fire from that cave. I took Wiley and Joe to cover me and we went over the crest on the right side, to a point where I could drop a couple grenades in the cave. They must have gone down quite a way, for when the grenades exploded there was just a very muffled "poof" on the surface. We waited a little while by the cave but nothing more came from it. We watched the boys from the Fourth and the Japs throwing grenades back and forth over the little ridge they were on. The marines soon killed the Japs, or drove them off, and we returned to the opposite side of the ridge, where we would have some protection from small arms and artillery fire.

We got a new lieutenant there that the replacement depot sent because we had lost ours. He was a big, brave, pleasant Irishman, a ninety-day wonder, and this was his first dose of combat. That night when the mortars started falling on us, he wanted to charge the Jap mortar positions. Some of us finally got him convinced that that wasn't a prudent thing to do at night. Their batteries were probably fifteen hundred or two thousand yards away, and there would be a lot of Jap machine guns and riflemen dug in between us and the mortars. If we had been lucky enough to get through those troops to the mortars, we would unquestionably have been so disorganized that we would have been as likely to shoot each other as the Japs.

In the daylight the lieutenant wanted us to charge over the crest and set up on the front face of the ridge. I told him I didn't think that would be a good idea, either. He said he thought there might be Japs over the ridge and we should go rout them out.

I was certain there would be hell to pay if we did that. Shuri was only a few hundred yards in front of us. I asked the lieutenant if it would be OK if I went over there and checked it out. That suited him.

Some of our men had been listening to the lieutenant and me talking. I asked if anyone wanted to go along, and one young rifleman said, "I'll go with you, Johnsey." How I wish I could remember his name. What he did might not sound like much in the warm glow of your parlor, but on Okinawa that day it was a very significant act. He had stuck his neck out a long fucking way and he knew it, but still he volunteered.

So over the ridge we went. Jap trenches had been dug back and forth all over the area. I don't think the Japs had been gone long because I could still smell them, literally, and the odor was very strong. The rifleman and I went quickly through all the trenches, trying always to be mindful of trip wires and areas likely to be trapped. He was a big help. Two of us could cover the ground faster and we could be on the watch to help each other, if need be. When we were sure there was nothing there, we hustled back over the ridge.

We had worked very hard in making a thorough search very quickly. I lay down on my back against the slope of the hill. Wiley came over and stood at my feet as he looked forward over the crest. He wanted to learn what we had found on the other side.

I was looking at Brown as I talked to him. Suddenly, there was a loud swishing noise as something passed by us very close, and his eyes widened. Almost simultaneously, a large round of artillery hit close in the valley behind us. Brown said, "Jesus Christ, Jim, that almost hit me in the face."

The round had been coming so nearly straight at his eyes that, even as fast as it was going, Brown could see it in flight.

It is odd how things that are nearest to tragedy when they happen sometimes become laughable when you recall them. I still giggle inanely when I think of Brown getting bug-eyed as a five-inch round of Jap artillery nearly hit him full in the face. Of course it would have killed us both, so I'm not laughing at Brown, I am laughing at us.

The little rifleman and I had barely gotten back from our two-man patrol of the south side of the ridge when the Jap artillery blew hell out of the place we had just left. If we had all gone over there and stayed, only a lucky few would have had any chance to survive. As it was, the poor lieutenant was killed, later. It looked as though he was shot in the arm. If so he either died of shock or the bullet that hit him in the arm continued into vital organs. It was a shame. He was a great fellow. If we could have kept him alive long enough for him to get some idea about the war to go along with his book learning, I know he would have made a good officer.

We found out that the big part of the Jap defenders of Shuri had either taken off or died. The trenches on the ridge in front of the town were empty. What was left was not the original strong line of defense. In the night another battalion of the Fifth Marines, the First, took over our positions and moved into Shuri with less trouble than they expected. I read about a marine officer raising the Confederate flag on Shuri, and I wonder how many of the marines who died making that possible for him were Confederates and how many were Union. I wonder how many were like me, born on one side and raised on the other, with a father from one side and a mother from the other. I wonder how many are like me, deathly ashamed of all the bastards in charge on both sides that ever allowed the tragedy of the Civil War to happen.

We went back over a few hills to the area near where our company mortars were set up and awaited our next assignment. It was such a relief to be able to stand up and walk around without the Jap machine guns and snipers working us over.

We drew new rations, including canned heat, tooth powder, and such, most precious of which was plenty of water. After a little while (the exact time period gets away from me again) we began another offensive.

The army on our left flank had advanced several hundred yards along the east coast. A plan was devised whereby we would move down the coast as far as possible and then turn, at right angles, to the west and send a pincer into the Jap area behind their lines in the central part of the island. The burden of being the point on this assignment fell on the First platoon of E-2-5.

When we had made the flanking movement into the Jap area and had advanced several hundred yards, we came to a rather prominent knob of land directly to our front. When "the man" said we should have a couple of strong points — that being machine guns on high ground — it seemed natural for me to say, "I think we can make it." I took my gunners and the guys that would go with us up to the top of the ridge on Hill 57. At least I was told it was Hill 57. I couldn't swear to that but I'll refer to it as such. To me it was just another hill.

We passed some caves on the reverse sides of some of the higher ground as we made our way to the crest. When we got to the top, some of us started to work the caves we had bypassed. One of them looked especially foreboding. The opening was a fairly large hole in the bank. You could see to the back of the cave, but there were tunnels going both ways, right and left, from the main opening. As we began dumping grenades into the cave we could hear the Japs inside working themselves into a frenzy. With each assault we made on the cave their frenzy increased.

Quite suddenly a black, acrid smoke started to roll thickly from the cave opening. I told the guys we had better back off some because it looked like something was going to blow. Before we could move more than a few yards, there was the biggest explosion I was ever near. One whole side of that pretty-big hill was blown completely away. It erupted like a small volcano and my men were right in the face of it.

I had been standing when the hill exploded. I was blown forward, flat on my belly. When all the ground that had been blown up settled back to earth, I tried quickly to assess the situation. In my back there was a tingling numbness but I seemed able to move all right in spite of it, so I started checking the men. Three of them were dead, two of them close to me on both sides.

I helped patch up all of them I could. One of them couldn't see, one's arm was mostly gone, one's leg was about gone from just below his knee, and one couldn't move from his waist down. Several more were wounded in a variety of ways and places.

The corpsman and I put them back together as best we could, and I went with them back to company headquarters to report. When I had accounted for my men the First Sergeant asked if I was turning in, too, and I said that I was. He asked what was wrong and added, "Need a rest?"

I said, "Hell, yes, I need a rest, but that's not why I'm turnin' in. I got hit in the side." As I was fully dressed and equipped, I imagine he wondered if I was just weary.

I started the trip back with my beat-up outfit. At each med station we would drop off a few and continue.

It had all happened in the late afternoon. As we went back to the aid stations and mobile hospitals it got later and later. About 2 or 3 A.M. we finally had taken care of all the boys. It was in a rear area field medical unit that I found myself the only one left. The doctor turned to me and asked, "What's your problem?"

I said, "I don't know, sir, but something is starting to hurt pretty bad in my back and side."

He told me to peel off my gear and he'd have a look. I was still wearing all my clothes, my pack (minus the shovel, since its handle had been broken in two by the big blow), and my cartridge belt, and I was carrying my carbine.

I laid down my weapon, took off the pack, cartridge belt, and my dungarees. My cartridge belt had one hole in it. The doc looked at me a moment and said, "Son, lie down on the stretcher on your belly and don't move until I tell you to."

For seven months I had done my best to take care of that bunch of kids and old man Brown. Sometimes pissed off at them for getting lazy or indifferent about what they needed to do, and most of the time so very proud of them. But however I felt, always trying to act with their best interests uppermost in my conscious efforts. I tried to teach them what they needed to know and to take care of them as best I could. I had done a pretty good job, too. I'd mothered them through some terribly tough spots without losing too many. Up to this time, that is, up to the hill I know as Hill 57. There I lost damn near all of them. I felt so helpless, so futile. As I lay down on the stretcher I took a very deep breath and fell sound asleep. I awakened slightly to the jiggling of someone carrying the stretcher and then I slept in fitful short snatches as the ambulance bounced its way back to an army field hospital. They unloaded me into one of the tents.

I awoke to the sound of someone laughing. It was a unique, very individual laughter and I was certain that I recognized it. Into the darkness I asked, "Anyone here from Nebraska?"

Back from the darkness came, "Who said Nebraska?"

"Kenny? Kenny Yant?" I asked.

"Yeah. Who is it?"

"Jim Johnston."

"My God, Jim. I look at all the incoming cards. I saw your name but your card said you were from Kentucky, so I didn't think it was you."

"The folks moved back to Kentucky after the war started, Ken. What are you doing here. Are you wounded?"

"No, Jim, I'm a medic. Where are you hit?"

I told him, in my side and my back. He said he'd take a look at me. It had been a long time before that, and was a long time after, that I was as glad to see anyone. He was a good friend from home. When I went to the operating room to have the steel cut out of me, Kenny went along. He stood by the operating table and held my hand. They had given me a local anaesthetic to deaden the pain while the doctor cut the shrapnel out of my side. As the surgeon was operating on the side of my body with his scalpel, the pain shot through me like a bolt of lightning. ("Uh oh! Hit a nerve.") My muscles jerked involuntarily. I still remember the feeling right after that, when Kenny's grip tightened on my hand.

I suppose it was in apprehension that the doctor would hit something like that again that I began to sweat quite profusely. A little nurse came over and wiped my face with a damp cloth. She said, "Don't sweat it, marine. The doc's about got it."

Her touch felt like an angel's. She was close enough that I could smell her. She smelled like Camay soap, the kind my mother always bought. All of a sudden I felt better.

As far as the war was concerned, my association with the Marine Corps was about over.

Kenny Yant went back with me to my sack in the ward tent. There I spent most of the next few days lying on my belly. Afterward Kenny would help me walk, a little farther each day.

I wrote V-mail to the folks from the hospital:

Dearest Mom and Dad,

Here it is June 5th and the story goes on. Haven't heard from you or anyone or been able to write for a little while but everything is still going fine. I am in the hospital now but will be out soon. I got a very little wound — nothing to worry about. It is just a scratch on my side and back. I'll only be in the hospital a couple days and then back to duty.

I saw Kenny Yant yesterday and it is wonderful to see someone from the old home town. He talks to me quite often and is a lot of fun.

I will close for this time and write again when I can.

God be with you til we meet again,

Jim

I never did tell Mom about the doc cutting the steel out of me. I just kept writing that all was well and the wounds were nothing but a scratch. I know the folks knew that something didn't exactly add up when I was still writing them from the hospital on June 21.

Dearest Mom and Dad,

June 21st and my heart is a little low. In spite of myself I write that. You know how it is — sometimes a person thinks too much.

I am still in the hospital but will probably go back either tomorrow or the next day. I am fine and all is well. I am hoping and praying that I can come home soon.

I have four little bronze battle stars in my South Pacific campaign bar now and a purple heart with a star.

If I'd been with my outfit (instead of in the hospital) last week I'd have made sergeant. Might have made it anyway but I doubt it. They don't give rates to guys in the hospital. It doesn't worry me, but I've been doing a sergeant's job for seven months and

would surely like to have gotten the rank to go with it. If I don't
make it here I'll never make it. They'll never advance my rate in a
new outfit where I'm unknown and unproven.

Be that as it may — it is of little consequence. [I write] mainly
to let you know that up to now I am OK.

Jim

When I wrote, "My heart is a little low," there were several reasons.
When I had left E Company with my wound, there were eleven men left
on the line in the first platoon (which originally consisted of three rifle
squads and two machine-gun squads). Those eleven were all that was
left of the original outfit and an unknown number of replacements.
Nine riflemen remained. As I recall, of my gunners (thirteen to begin
with and an estimated six replacements), there were two remaining.
Two. One of them had been shot through the leg and had returned to
duty to be wounded again, and the other (it was reported to me) was
later killed in action.

I have read accounts that describe machine gunners as support
troops. When I do so, I begin to question the writers' credibility, or at
least their judgment. I know they were either never where I was or they
are careless about honoring the facts. I served enough duty as a scout to
know firsthand the perils of that job. I watched enough riflemen die in
front of me to ingrain the deep respect I have for them. But there were a
great many days when I set our machine guns out on top of the ground
in salients and on hilltops with no one but the enemy in front of us. And
it was *every* long, fucking lonesome night that we manned those positions. Is experience like that grounds for lumping us off with the support
troops? When there was *nobody* between you and the Japs all night, every night, it was a different ball game entirely — different from anywhere else.

While I had been caring for the wounded on Hill 57, I noticed that the
serial numbers on the dog tags of some of the dead, who were recent replacements, were 250,000 less than mine. Serial numbers were a big
deal in the corps. Supposedly, they indicated how long you had been

there. The size of a serial number didn't have any significance to me. Much more important to me was what you were, where you were, and what you had been doing. I think the corps assigned numbers by the batch to certain areas, which might account for men with lower numbers getting to the war so much later. There were also fairly large groups of men in ROTC programs, and the like, who were given serial numbers even though they were a long way from being marines.

I had been in the hospital a week or so after the surgeons had removed the shrapnel inside me. I was quietly lying on my sack absorbing the peace and quiet. There were a lot of wounded soldiers in the ward tent. One afternoon a mouthy first sergeant from some outfit in the First Marine Regiment was admitted to the ward. He had come to the hospital for tests to see if he had worms. He didn't know I was a marine, and I never told him. He talked too much and too loud, so he wasn't making points with the wounded army boys. I didn't feel like getting into that discord, however, so I just kept my mouth shut.

In a couple of days another marine from the first sergeant's unit came into the ward, and the sergeant asked the boy what was happening. The young marine told him he thought their outfit was going to relieve some unit of the Fifth on the ridge. The sergeant said, "Yeah, whenever the Fifth runs into something, the First always has to relieve them."

Before I had time to think, I said, "Bullshit, sergeant. Where the fuck were you people after the first few days on Peleliu? Weeks after you had all left, I got hit working the hills you were supposed to take."

I immediately regretted what I'd said. The sergeant had been badly out of line, but I served no useful purpose in taking exception to his absurd remark. I didn't need any more conflict right then, and I'm sure the sergeant didn't either.

He muttered something about the casualties they'd had, but he was pretty quiet after that. I was ashamed I'd spouted off. I have never been able to make myself feel better by making someone else feel bad. I wish I had just said something to the effect that we always felt the same about them. There were so many good men in the First Marines. A lot of them died, a lot were old friends of mine. One of them who lived through Peleliu told me one time, after a few drinks, how he hated it that we had had to spend so many tough weeks in combat on Peleliu after the First Marines had left. Maybe the sergeant felt the same way. I was ashamed then of the way I had hopped on him. I still am.

He left the hospital soon after that. I imagine he went back for the few days — the few nasty days — that were left of the war. I hope he made it through.

While I was in the hospital, one of our anti-aircraft batteries of 90MM guns somehow got out of synchronism and fired a few rounds into the hospital area. The shrapnel cut holes in the tent where I was recovering. I thought what a wicked joke it would be to fight the Japs for two years and then die in the hospital from rounds of our own anti-aircraft.

When I checked out of the hospital, I reported back to battalion head-quarters. Instead of being sent on to E Company, I was taken to a casual company to await transportation home. While I was there, some of the people from my old outfit came to see me. They told me that if I would volunteer to return to E Company and stay for the next campaign, I would probably be gunny — top NCO — of our platoon, and my cobber Utter would have the company. It sounded good.

I damn near stayed. Even knowing that I would almost certainly be there forever, my allegiance to my men and the corps had become so strong that I damn near stayed.

Only thoughts of my folks tipped my decision in favor of going home. I could hold Mother and Dad in my arms and tell them how much I loved them. I could then tell them what it was that I would be going back to, tell them the cold truth. Then I could return to hit Japan and die, and all would be OK.

I was sure I had too much experience for the corps to allow me to leave for good. I was sure they would bring me back to the Pacific, certainly for something as critical as hitting the Japanese homeland. And that was fine by me, if I could first see home and the folks once more, if I could say goodbye and tell the girls, "Hey, baby, long time no come see."

The division went to China. When I had arrived overseas, I had two friends who had seen old-time China duty and they were great. I would have given the proverbial "left one" to get a chance at China duty. If I had been lucky enough to live through it, there would have been some tall tales to tell.

I stayed on Okinawa until the campaign was over, but I never went back into the lines. I was there on the Fourth of July, when all our batteries of big artillery turned loose to celebrate our Independence Day. I left for home shortly thereafter, around the middle of July.

I didn't write the folks that I was coming home. I figured if I got home it would be great, but if I wrote I was coming and didn't make it, everyone would be morbid. I waited until I was in the States and called home to say I'd be there in three days, God willing.

If I'd had any idea how things were going to turn out I'd have stayed on Okinawa instead of coming home. The way it was, the United States dropped the atomic bombs on Japan, and the war was over before I was due to return to the Pacific Theater.

9. Home

FROM OKINAWA I boarded a slow transport and sailed to Pearl Harbor, where we lay at anchor for a few days. I volunteered to take some working parties ashore to load supplies, mainly so that I could say I had done duty in Hawaii, but also as a way to break up the monotony of staying aboard ship, doing nothing.

When our ship was nearing sight of the American mainland, the ship's command notified the troops, and we all climbed to some vantage point where we could see the Golden Gate Bridge as soon as possible. Very impressive, very moving. I had been gone from my homeland for twenty-five months.

There was a band playing on the dock, and I wondered what celebration we had stumbled onto. It was difficult for me to swallow when I learned they were playing for us. We weren't used to much fanfare.

When we went ashore, we were almost immediately granted freedom of the base, to hit the stateside PX and cafe. We could hardly believe that whatever was on the menu was ours to eat and drink. Three of us ordered twelve bottles of chocolate milk and quaffed them in no time flat. Then we started to eat.

It was later at that same station, Treasure Island, that we went before a briefing officer. He was a captain and he made quite a lengthy precautionary reorientation lecture about dealing with the civilian world. One thing that he said tickled me. First, he said that while we were away, we had built a dream world out of home, but in reality it was just part of the same old world. We needed to be ready for many disappointments.

Then he added that the blonde who lived down the street had probably gotten married — and worse than that, she'd moved.

I went back to Nebraska for three weeks or so of convalescent leave and then reported for duty at Moffet Field, Mountain View, California. Because of the length of time I had been part of E Company, and the combat experience I had, the company had confidence in me. I carried some weight there. At least half of the old guys who had made it through in E Company owed their continued existence to me and a couple of other guys like me. But when I left my old outfit, I hadn't yet gotten the rating that I had earned as a section leader. So I was just another corporal among a bunch of new acquaintances, among a bunch of strangers who didn't know me from Adam. When I was transferred to the detachment at the Naval Air Station at Moffet Field, I was assigned to a guard unit where I'd be standing post four hours on and four hours off, like a private.

Jesus wept! The Marine Corps was at it again.

I had gotten my ass shot up and seen men killed all around me, leading them into places the devil himself wouldn't go. I had done the job the Marine Corps told me to do, and done it well. They even attested to that fact by a letter of commendation I received, signed by General Roy Geiger. I had given them more than two years of faithful service in the Asiatic-Pacific Theater, but that had ended.

Now who would give me the grade, or the pay, or the consideration I had earned? Nobody in the corps would do so. Once more they had given me the short end of the stick. But there wasn't any changing it and I was resigned to that fact.

My post was in a little wooden shack about the size of a two-holer outhouse. It was located on a perimeter road on the extreme outskirts of an underground ammo dump. Talk about being in the boonies! I was issued a carbine with no live ammo. It was about as useless and absurd a position as you could find in this world. It certainly was not a fitting place to assign a shot-up old section leader. You could tell how critical the guard post was to the corps from the fact that they didn't even issue me live ammo. If someone attacked me, I could hit him over the head with my empty carbine.

Out there on post the first day, I had taken off my cover[1] and leaned the empty carbine up in the corner of the little shack. I was sitting on one of the brace boards inside the shack when I heard something on the road.

Through a crack in the boards of the wall, I saw a jeep slowly, quietly approaching the rear of the shack. The gunnery sergeant driving the jeep was sneaking up on me. I didn't want to risk being seen jumping around after my gear like he'd caught me at something. So I stepped out the door of the shack without my cover or weapon — and casually hailed him. "Hi ya, Gunny. What's going on?"

I knew what was going on. He was wearing an arm band lettered OD. This noncombatant gunnery sergeant was playing officer of the day, and he was looking for someone who would snap to for him. Well, he'd come to the wrong place. Neither he nor the situation rated shit as far as I was concerned.

The gunny was flabbergasted, completely taken aback by my attitude and conduct. "I'm inspecting the guard," he said.

"If you're looking for something exciting, you'll have to go somewhere besides this graveyard, Gunny."

You could see he had decided I wasn't going to play his game, and I guess he was reconciled to it. Still, he said, "If the real OD comes around you'd better report your post in a military manner. He expects the guard to go by the book."

"Then you might tell him in my outfit I was a section leader. I stood sergeant of the guard. If the motherfucker wants to operate by the book, that's what I should be doing now, and some private with a billy club should be watching these piles of concrete."

When he left I wondered if he would put me on report. I didn't really care. I'd joined the marines to help fight a war, and we'd done a pretty good job. The war was over and I didn't want to play their peacetime games. I hoped that I could find something more worthwhile to do than spit-shining boondockers and scrubbing 782 gear.[2] It was time now to start telling myself not to kill whoever got in my way, then praying that I'd listen.

I guess some of my thoughts must have shown in my face, because that was the last I ever heard from the gunnery sergeant. I'm sure he realized that I knew a dozen ways I could get rid of him, and no one would ever be the wiser. Of course I would never have considered doing anything like that, but the sergeant didn't know as much. All he knew was that, like Lawrence of Arabia, I had "sailed many ships and killed many men," and that I wasn't happy with his whole operation. I'm sure the gunny thought it would be more productive, and probably far safer, to try his chickenshit routine on some greener marine.

The war was over. The point system had been devised to start discharging marines who were in the corps only for the duration of the national emergency. When I reported to the station that handled the point system, I found that the corps had lost all my medical records. Down in the sea or up in flames, either way they were gone. My only medical records were the notices of my wounds that the War Department had sent my parents. The folks had kept those notices in their safe.

When I knew the date I would be discharged, I called home. Dad once more scrounged enough gas coupons to drive the old Oldsmobile out to pick me up. Except in my dreams — and in memories of the marines I had known — my association with the corps was over.

One thing I wanted to do before leaving California was to pay my respects to the family of Jack Howell. He had been a replacement on Okinawa, one of the few that I had gotten to know well. He had been a good kid and a solid marine.

He was from a good family, who were very close. He had showed me a picture of his classy Mercury convertible, which his dad was taking care of until Jack got home.

Jack had been killed in the hills toward the south end of Okinawa. The night I went to see his family at their home in Pasadena, his mother answered the door, and I told her Jack Howell had been a close friend of mine. Mrs. Howell introduced me to Jack's sister and brother. His mother told me, "Jack's father died of a heart attack when they brought him word that Jack had been killed on Okinawa."

It was a melancholy place. I told Mrs. Howell her son had been brave and honorable. I hoped that might be some consolation.

When I was leaving she offered me the souvenirs her son had sent home including a fancy Jap sword. I sometimes wish I had taken the items and kept them as mementos of my association with Jack, but at that time they were just Japanese tokens to me, and I had all the memories of the Japs I wanted.

When I left the Howells, I joined my father in the car outside, where he had waited. I put my arms around him and wept in the futility of deep sorrow.

I went back to Nebraska, but not back to life as it had been. I had given the corps the best I had, and it had given me a new set of values. I didn't give a damn about going back to college, or trying to become what our society seems to think of as a success. Wealth and influence had lost all significance. In the dark corners of my mind, the only power under God that meant anything to me came out of the bore of a .30-06 — or if you were close enough, a .45. Those dark corners are still there.

At the time I got out of the corps, what I hoped for most was a place where I could be alone and at peace. However, it wasn't long before I found that the Marine Corps had left me with something besides a desire to escape the world, something I don't really understand. It's a feeling, like one of obligation, toward the fucking corps. Can you imagine that? The sons of bitches had short-sheeted me at every association. And yet . . . we had been through too much together. I'm a part of their history, good or bad, whether they like it or not. They can't disavow me. But it works both ways. I can't abandon them either.

It seems entirely inappropriate and undesirable that I should just live out the days. I keep looking for a hill to assault, hoping for a hill to assault, and then another and another until there are no more hills. Or no more me.

Notes

1. MY INTRODUCTION TO THE CORPS

1. Mother had written a letter and put it in my shaving kit for me to find when I was on my way. It was filled with love and consoling thoughts.

2. Boot camp was Marine Corps basic training. The term referred both to the site at which training took place and to the period of time spent there, that being the weeks following enlistment and preceding regular duty.

3. To a sailor or a marine, about anything you can stand on is "the deck."

4. Dad and I had played with the idea of trying to communicate with one another telepathically while we were separated.

2. ON TO AUSTRALIA

1. Boonies was an abbreviated form of the term boondocks. Boondocks are any remote or rough, unpopulated area.

2. China marines who had done duty in China prior to World War II.

3. NEW GUINEA AND THE JUNGLE

1. Alice was Mother's sister.

2. Lefty was a good friend from home. He was killed in a bombing raid on the Ploesti oil field in Romania.

4. NEW BRITAIN: A LOOK AT THE MONKEY SHOW

1. Shavetail, second John, and second looie were all terms used to describe second lieutenants.

2. U.S. Marines are called leathernecks because early corps uniforms included a leather collar designed to defend against saber strokes to the neck.

3. Survey was a marine term for the process of exchanging an article damaged or worn out for a new issue.

4. A TS (tough-shit) card was a fanciful item meaning bad luck. When distressing circumstances befell a marine, he was advised to "get his TS card punched."

6. HELL HAS A NAME: PELELIU

1. Our commanders had told us that we could expect heavy casualties but that we would be finished, dead or alive, in three days. That suited us fine — do it and have it over with, good or bad, in a hurry — but it didn't work out like that.

2. *Banzai* was a term shouted by Japanese soldiers during some attacks, roughly translated "to the death."

3. Cobber was the Australian term for a close friend. Your cobber was your buddy.

4. A marine filled with an enthusiastic sense of duty or purpose was said to be gung ho. The Chinese phrase means "pull together."

5. A half-D was an Australian halfpenny coin.

6. A watch I had sent home for repair was lost or stolen in the mail.

7. Cornelia was an old friend of my dad's family; E.P. was the mailman; Gaylord was my cousin.

7. RETURN TO PAVUVU

1. Attacking with a fragmentation grenade.

2. Mare Island was an infamous stateside naval prison.

3. Joe had taken over one of the squads until a more senior man, one of the casualties, returned from the hospital.

4. I made corporal on Pavuvu and was given command of a section of machine guns — twelve men.

8. OKINAWA: THE LAST INVASION

1. Mike was a good friend from home who was in the corps, Second Division.

2. The folks had sold the farm in Kentucky and were moving back to Nebraska.

3. Standard issue semiautomatic rifle for World War II–era riflemen.

9. HOME

1. A marine refers to his hat or cap as "cover."

2. Webbed gear such as a cartridge belt or pack.

Bibliography

As my work is a personal account rather than a historical narrative, a bibliography may not be necessary or appropriate. However, at the suggestion of some whose opinions I value highly, I have drawn up a brief list.

With the exceptions of Catton's moving history of the American Civil War, which concerns matters outside the realm of my experience, and Markham's anthology of beautiful and timeless poetry, the references listed here are not intended as suggestions for further reading. These materials have served primarily to give me a sense of perspective as to how my experience relates to that of others. In some instances I have used the books to check such matters as spellings and casualty counts and, on occasion, to jog my memory regarding matters mostly arcane or largely inconsequential.

Berry, Henry. *Semper Fi, Mac.* New York: Berkley Books, 1983.

Catton, Bruce. *This Hallowed Ground.* New York: Pocket Books, 1961.

Feifer, George. *Tennozan: The Battle of Okinawa and the Atomic Bomb.* New York: Ticknor & Fields, 1992.

Inenaga, Saburo. *The Pacific War, 1931–1945: A Critical Perspective on Japan's Role in World War II.* New York: Pantheon Books, 1978.

Jones, James. *WWII: A Chronicle of Soldiering.* New York: Ballantine Books, 1976.

Manchester, William. *Goodbye, Darkness: A Memoir of the Pacific War.* Boston: Little, Brown, 1980.

Markham, Edwin, et al. *Anthology of the World's Best Poems.* New York: William H. Wise, 1948.

McMillan, George. *The Old Breed: A History of the First Marine Division in World War II.* Washington DC: Infantry Journal Press, 1949.

Muster Roll of Officers and Enlisted Men of the U.S. Marine Corps: Second Battalion, Fifth Marines, First Marine Division, Fleet Marine Force. September 1–30, 1944, inclusive; June 1–30, 1945, inclusive. Washington DC: History and Museums Division, Headquarters, U.S. Marine Corps.

Ross, Bill D. *Peleliu: Tragic Triumph: The Untold Story of the Pacific War's Forgotten Battle.* New York: Random House, 1991.

Shaw, Henry I., Jr., Bernard C. Nalty, and Edwin T. Turnbladh. *Central Pacific Drive: History of U.S. Marine Corps Operations in World War II*, vol. 3. Washington DC: Historical Branch, G-3 Division, HQMC, 1966.

Sledge, E. B. *With the Old Breed at Peleliu and Okinawa.* Novato CA: Presidio Press, 1981.